Children's
ANCIENT WORLD
Encyclopedia

Author: K.M. Santon

Consultant: Fiona Waters

This edition produced by Atlantic Publishing

First published by Parragon in 2009

Parragon
Queen Street House
4 Queen Street
Bath BA1 1HE, UK

ISBN 978-1-4075-7380-9

Printed in Indonesia

Children's
ANCIENT WORLD
Encyclopedia

Discover the secrets of the past

K.M. Santon

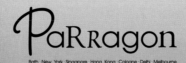

Bath · New York · Singapore · Hong Kong · Cologne · Delhi · Melbourne

CONTENTS

The Ancient World

1   Chaco Canyon
2   Tenochtitlan
3   Teotihuacan
4   Palenque
5   Sipan
6   Machu Picchu
7   Hadrian's Wall
8   Stonehenge
9   Lascaux
10   Rome
11   Pompeii and Herculaneum
12   Knossos
13   Troy
14   Mycenae
15   Athens
16   Sparta
17   Leptis Magna
18   Carthage
19   Memphis
20   Thebes
21   Great Zimbabwe
22   Jericho
23   Ur
24   Persepolis
25   Babylon
26   Mohenjo-Daro
27   Nineveh
28   Uluru

North America

Atlantic Ocean

South America

Pacific Ocean

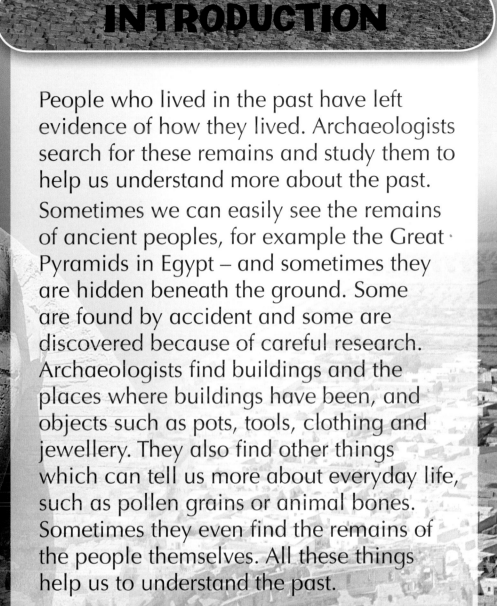

INTRODUCTION

People who lived in the past have left evidence of how they lived. Archaeologists search for these remains and study them to help us understand more about the past.

Sometimes we can easily see the remains of ancient peoples, for example the Great Pyramids in Egypt – and sometimes they are hidden beneath the ground. Some are found by accident and some are discovered because of careful research. Archaeologists find buildings and the places where buildings have been, and objects such as pots, tools, clothing and jewellery. They also find other things which can tell us more about everyday life, such as pollen grains or animal bones. Sometimes they even find the remains of the people themselves. All these things help us to understand the past.

EARLY EUROPE

Humans have evolved over millions of years and experts believe that *Homo sapiens*, our direct ancestors, began to inhabit Europe about 35,000 years ago. At first they were hunter-gatherers, moving in search of food, living in caves or in shelters made from wood and animal skins. After many thousands of years they began to farm and build settlements. By about 2300 BC, metals such as bronze, and later iron, began to be used to make tools, weapons and everyday items, many of which have been found by archaeologists digging in the soil. Many early peoples also left stone monuments, which were often enormous, as well as traces of the places where they lived.

Ice Age hunters

During the last Ice Age, which began about 100,000 years ago, large parts of the world were covered with ice, but there were colder and warmer periods. Sea levels rose and fell and people began to move around the world, following the animals they hunted.

Top Fact

- Ice Age people knew how to make fire. In Chauvet Cave in southern France, archaeologists have found traces of fires and places where flaming torches smoked against the walls.

People in Europe

One type of early people, called Neanderthals, seem to have been particularly good at living in cold areas. When the climate warmed up, *Homo sapiens*, our ancestors, started to take over areas where Neanderthals had lived. The bones of Neanderthal people were found in this cave in Croatia.

Neanderthals

The Neanderthal's skull is longer and flatter than that of a modern human and the bone above the eyes is more prominent. Neanderthals were smaller and more stockily built than we are today.

Tools

Early people made tools by chipping flint and other types of stone so that a sharp point was created. This flint axe head was found in England. Experts think that it is more than 100,000 years old.

Did You Know?

Experts think that Homo sapiens originated in Africa but had spread to every continent except Antarctica by 9000 BC.

An Ice Age cave painting from Lascaux in France

Paintings in caves

The earliest works of art were created by people about 30,000 years ago. Paintings were made on the walls of caves in western Europe, deep underground. They often show animals and scenes of hunting. Sculptures of animals or people have also been found.

Nobody knows for sure why such beautiful art should exist in places that are so dark and difficult to reach. They may be linked to bringing good fortune to hunters.

Megaliths in Europe

Farming spread from the Middle East into Europe about 6000 years ago. This period in European history is called the Neolithic period. During the Neolithic period huge stone monuments, called megaliths, were built in many parts of western Europe. Many of these monuments are older than the pyramids in Egypt.

Stonehenge in south-west England

Stone monuments

Stonehenge is the best-known megalithic ('big stone') monument but there are many others in France, Ireland and Britain. Carnac, in northern France, is the biggest megaltihic site in Europe, with about 3000 standing stones. Nobody knows why megalithic monuments were built, but they were probably connected to religion.

Carnac

Top Facts

- Neolithic houses have been found on Scotland's Orkney Islands. The furniture was made from stone.

- People were buried at some, but not all, megalithic monuments. They may have been used as burial sites for hundreds of years.

Megalithic sites

Callanish • • Orkney

IRELAND • • BRITAIN

Newgrange •

• Arbor Low

Stonehenge • • Avebury

West Kennet •

Carnac • FRANCE Alps

Puy de Paulhiac •

Did You Know?

In September 1991 two climbers found a body in the Alps. The man turned out to have died over 5000 years ago. He had been shot with an arrow. Some of his belongings were found – such as a quiver and a backpack – and even his clothes survived. He is now known as The Iceman.

The Bronze Age

The period historians call the Bronze Age began in about 2300 BC. At first only a few tools were made from metal. Most people still used stone, but this gradually changed.

Copper and tin were needed to make bronze but these metals were not found everywhere. Trade developed as people exchanged other things for the metal they needed, and settlements grew larger. People made weapons such as swords from bronze because it was stronger than tin or copper.

A Bronze Age shield

Iron Age tribes in Europe

During the last centuries BC, people across Europe began to use iron to make weapons and tools. Archaeologists have found a large number of iron weapons, such as swords and spearheads, so they think the Iron Age must have been a warlike time.

Tribes and peoples

The Iron Age people left no written records of their own, but the Greeks – and later the Romans – knew about them. The Romans called the Iron Age tribes barbarians and thought they were uncivilized. Today the ancestors of these Iron Age people are called the Celts.

There were many separate Iron Age tribes led by chieftains who often fought each other. Eventually the Roman armies defeated most of these tribes and many Celtic areas, such as modern Britain and France, became parts of the Roman Empire.

Top Facts

- The Hittites, who lived in what is modern Turkey, were the first people to learn how to make iron objects in about 1500 BC.

- Although iron was used to make tools and weapons, many decorative items were made from bronze, which was an easier metal to work with.

The defences of this English Iron Age hill fort, called Maiden Castle, are easy to see.

Villages and towns

Iron age people lived in lots of different kinds of settlements, from isolated round farmhouses to larger settlements such as Biskupin in Poland. We know that this large village was made entirely of wood in 738–737 BC because the timber can be dated. Here you can see a reconstruction of the walls of Biskupin.

An oil lamp from Halstatt

Mines

Iron Age people dug mines, such as the Halstatt salt mines in Austria. Leather backpacks used by Iron Age miners have been found there.

Peat bog remains

Many Iron Age remains, including people, have been found in peat bogs. The most famous body, from Denmark, is known as Tollund Man. Despite looking very peaceful, he had actually been strangled. He was probably sacrificed to the gods.

Did You Know?

An important person would wear a heavy gold ring called a torc around their neck. Some warriors went into battle completely naked except for a torc.

ANCIENT EGYPT

About 5000 years ago, a great civilization began to grow up along the River Nile in Egypt. It lasted for 3000 years and during this time some of the most famous structures known to man were built. As well as these great monuments, the Egyptians left behind many everyday objects and wall paintings, which help us to understand how they lived, and the more mysterious mummies that were so important to them when they died.

The River Nile

The River Nile flooded every year and left layers of rich soil on its banks. The Egyptians grew crops on this fertile land, and also fished in the river. Egyptians called their county 'Kemet', which means 'black land', because of the rich dark colour of the soil.

Ancient Egypt

The Ancient Egyptian civilization lasted from about 3100 BC to 30 BC, when Egypt became part of the Roman Empire. The main periods of its history are called the Old, Middle and New Kingdoms. These periods are divided into dynasties – families of rulers.

Did You Know?

Everyone helped at harvest time, including women and children. Slaves and criminals were sometimes made to help, as were units of the army.

A wall painting from a tomb shows Egyptians ploughing the land and sowing seeds.

Settlements by the river

Towns and villages grew up along the Nile, between the river and the desert. The earliest city was Memphis, in the north of the country.

Ordinary Egyptians lived in small houses made from mud bricks. Small windows and an outdoor kitchen helped to keep their houses cool. Richer people had larger houses with a courtyard in the centre, and often a garden with a pond and trees.

The remains of Memphis

Farming and food

Wall paintings, written records and remains found by archaeologists tell us a great deal about farming and what the Egyptains ate. Farmers used hoes to turn the ground, as well as simple ploughs drawn by cows. They grew wheat and barley and kept a few animals such as cattle, sheep, goats, geese and ducks. Bread was the main food but people also ate vegetables, fruit, fish and meat. They seem to have particularly enjoyed beans, chickpeas and lentils, as well as garlic and onions. They liked lettuce and cucumbers, too, and everyone loved eating dates. Farmers also grew flax for making linen cloth.

Did You Know?
Only rich people ate a lot of meat. It could not be kept fresh for long because of the heat.

The kingdoms

Two separate kingdoms grew up along the River Nile, known as Upper and Lower Egypt. Lower Egypt was in the north around the Nile delta, and Upper Egypt stretched southwards for hundreds of kilometres.

Becoming one country

In about 3100 BC, King Narmer of Upper Egypt conquered Lower Egypt and united the two kingdoms. A joint capital city was created at Memphis, near the Nile delta. Rulers now wore a double crown, made up of Lower Egypt's red crown and King Narmer's white one.

A palette showing King Narmer, wearing the pointed white crown of Lower Egypt, defeating his enemies.

Figures from an Old Kingom tomb

The Old Kingdom

The period we call the Old Kingdom began in about 2680 BC, when the Third Dynasty (or family of rulers) controlled Egypt. The kings were powerful, ruling their huge country with the help of local governors. This period lasted about 500 years. Finally, King Pepi II ruled for so long that all his sons died before him. The governors then began a struggle for power that lasted many years.

The Middle Kingdom

The Middle Kingdom began in about 2055 BC. Egypt was peaceful again and the country grew richer as trade increased. The rulers of the Twelfth Dynasty conquered Egypt's neighbour Nubia (now called Sudan). However, eventually the power of the kings began to fade and by 1750 BC a people called the Hyksos had invaded Egypt and begun to occupy the north of the country.

The New Kingdom

In about 1550 BC, King Ahmose I managed to defeat the Hyksos invaders and drive them out of Egypt. There followed a period of about 500 years when Egypt had strong and stable government. This period is called the New Kingdom. Trade grew once again and Egypt conquered new territories using its newly created professional army. The kings became rich and built many magnificent temples and tombs.

Time Line

c. 3100 BC
Egypt unified

c. 2680 BC
The Old Kingdom

c. 2055 BC
The Middle Kingdom

c. 1550 BC
The New Kingdom

c. 31 BC
Egypt becomes part of the Roman Empire

The tomb of Ti at Saqqara dates from the Old Kingdom.

Death and the Afterlife

The Ancient Eyptians believed that there was an Afterlife, a new world where they would go when they died. They spent a lot of time preparing everything they would need for the journey.

Preparing for the journey

Egyptians thought that the most important parts of the spirit needed the physical body to survive after death, so it had to be preserved. There were also funeral ceremonies that needed to be completed, and people had to be accompanied by things they might use in the Afterlife. Then the spirit's journey could begin.

Top Facts

- People dreaded dying away from Egypt because the correct funeral ceremonies would not be performed.

- Funerals ended with a feast at home. There might even be acrobats and dancing girls.

A dead person might be buried with small wooden statues called shabti figures. It was thought that these would act as servants for them in the Afterlife.

The journey

The dead person had to be judged before being admitted to the next world, but before reaching the place of judgement a dangerous journey had to be undertaken. For example, 12 gateways guarded by monsters had to be passed. Spells were used to protect the dead person against these dangers.

Judgement

Eventually, the dead person reached the Hall of the Two Truths, where the heart was weighed against all the things the person had done when alive. This was a very tense moment as success meant the person could pass into the next world, the ideal version of Egypt, and live forever. Failure meant that the Devourer of the Dead would eat the heart and the person would not survive at all.

Anubis

The god Anubis weighs a heart.

Mummies

In order for someone to live happily in the Afterlife their body had to be preserved. These preserved bodies are called mummies.

Making a mummy

Embalming was a way of preserving the body so that it didn't rot. It was a skilled job, and the whole process took about 70 days. The body was taken to the 'Beautiful House' shortly after death. This was usually on the west bank of the Nile, away from areas where people lived.

Top Facts

- The heart was left in the body so that it could be weighed in the Afterlife; it was the most important organ.

- If a person had been injured in life, maybe losing a limb, they would be mummified with a false one in place so that the body was complete.

Did You Know?

Modern scientists used to have to unwrap mummies so they could study them. Now they are inspected using a scanner, which can see through the wrappings.

Removing the organs

The embalmers removed some organs – the lungs, liver, intestines, stomach and brain. These organs, except for the brain, were put in containers called canopic jars and buried with the mummy. Here (left) we can see the lid of one of the jars from the tomb of Tutankhamun. After the organs were removed, the body was filled with temporary stuffing and covered in a salt called natron to dry it out. About 40 days later, the body was washed, dried and given its final stuffing.

The Egyptians mummified some animals, too, especially those linked to the gods. This is a crocodile, the symbol of the god Sobek.

Bandaging

Once the mummified body was dried, it was carefully wrapped in bandages, starting with the fingers and toes. Jewellery and lucky charms were placed between the layers of linen to protect the mummy. Each layer was covered in perfumes, oils and resins. Over time these became solid. Finally, a decorative mask was placed over the head of the mummy and funeral ceremonies were carried out. Then the mummy was placed in its coffin and taken for burial.

This mummy was discovered at Fayoum, south of modern Cairo.

The first royal tombs

Tombs were important as they were a way for the dead person to be remembered. This was necessary if a spirit was to survive in the Afterlife.

The first tombs

Before the period called the Old Kingdom, structures called mastabas were built on top of the underground tombs of kings and nobles. These rectangular buildings had a flat roof and were made of mud bricks. Mastabas varied in size according to the importance of the person buried beneath.

Step pyramids

In about 2660 BC, the second king of the Third Dynasty, Djoser, had a new kind of tomb built at Saqqara. It looked like a pile of six mastabas, each one smaller than the one below. But it was square and built of stone; today it is called the Step Pyramid.

Top Facts
- The Step Pyramid was the first building in the world to be built entirely from stone.
- The pyramids at Giza are the largest and best known but there are over 100 pyramids in Egypt.

The Step Pyramid is about 60 metres tall.

The first real pyramids

Many kings after Djoser followed his example. Snefru, the first ruler of the Fourth Dynasty, built two pyramids called the Bent Pyramid (the sides are not straight) and the Red Pyramid. Archaeologists think Snefru was buried in the Red Pyramid.

The Bent Pyramid

Inside a pyramid

The pyramid of Unas is now a ruin, but inside there survives a burial chamber with writing carved into the walls.

How were the pyramids built?

We do not know for certain how the pyramids were built. It is most likely that a ramp was built around the pyramid itself, and that the huge stones were dragged up it. Once the pyramid was complete the ramp would have been broken up, starting at the top.

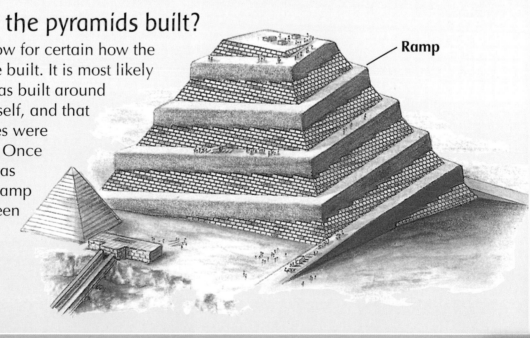

Ramp

The pyramids at Giza

Three great kings of the Old Kingdom built huge pyramids at Giza, on the west side of the River Nile, not far from their capital city, Memphis. The biggest, which was the tallest building in the world for thousands of years, belonged to King Khufu.

The Great Pyramid

King Khufu built his enormous tomb in about 2580 BC. It was never intended that people should enter the pyramids after the king's burial, and so the entrance was blocked. Historians think that King Khufu was buried with many valuable things, but we will never know because the pyramid, like all the others, had been robbed of its contents by 1000 BC.

The other two big pyramids at Giza belong to Khufu's son and grandson, Khafre and Menkaure.

Top Facts

- Khufu's Great Pyramid contains over 2.3 million blocks of limestone.
- Khafre's Pyramid looks taller than the Great Pyramid because it stands on slightly higher ground.

Menkaure's pyramid

Khafre's pyramid

Khufu's pyramid

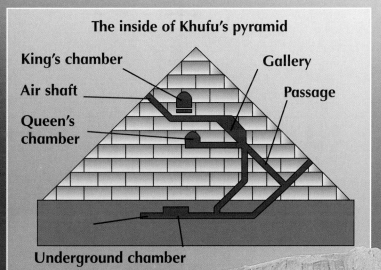

The inside of Khufu's pyramid

King's chamber

Air shaft

Queen's chamber

Gallery

Passage

Underground chamber

The mysterious sphinx

The huge sculpture called the Sphinx sits near Khafre's pyramid and was probably built at the same time. It has a lion's body but a human head, which is probably a portrait of the king.

The sphinx

Did You Know?

Most of the people who built the pyramids were not slaves. They would have been ordinary people, probably farmers, 'paying' their taxes by working for the king some of the time.

Decorating tombs

Many rich people had elaborate tombs built for them. These tombs were important for the journey to the Afterlife. The contents of the tombs tell us much about daily life in Ancient Egypt.

Burial places

Someone who was wealthy enough would build an underground tomb on the west bank of the River Nile. Tombs might consist of just one room, a burial chamber for the coffin. But if their owners were very rich, they might have several rooms. There could also be several coffins, one fitting inside another, all fitting inside a large stone outer coffin called a sarcophagus.

Top Facts
- People began preparing their tombs when they were still quite young and fit. It could take years.
- Models showing aspects of everyday life were often included in tombs, particularly during the Middle Kingdom.

Craftsmen

The village of Deir el-Medina was on the west bank of the Nile opposite Thebes. This was where the skilled craftsmen who built the tombs of the kings lived in the New Kingdom. On their days off, they worked for other wealthy people or created their own tombs. Since they were the best artists and carvers in Egypt, their tombs are especially beautiful. In this carving, two men are shown making a sculpture.

This model of a woman making bread came from a tomb.

Decoration

Tomb walls were often covered in paintings, or carvings and writing. These weren't only for decoration, but were important for life in the next world. A painting of someone enjoying a party, for example, would ensure that they would do this in the Afterlife. A scene showing breadmaking would show the tomb owner how to go about baking bread.

No matter how old, ill or injured the tomb owners were when they died, they were always shown as young, good-looking and fit in their tombs. This was to ensure that they would be physically perfect in the Afterlife.

The tomb of the nobleman Sennedjem was decorated with colourful paintings.

Did You Know?
You had to have money to have a tomb constructed. Poorer people were not mummified and were buried directly in the sand.

Religion and the temple

The Ancient Egyptians believed in many different gods and goddesses. Worshipping the gods was an important part of everyday life.

The gods

Some of the many gods were linked to particular tribes or villages, but others were eventually worshipped all over Egypt — though they often had one special temple.

Most of the gods governed a particular part of the world or life, for example Horus was the god of the sky and Thoth was the god of knowledge. They could be responsible for more than one thing, for example Hathor was a mother goddess but was also linked to music, dance, love and the sky.

What did gods look like?

Many gods were associated with a particular animal, and could be shown either as that animal or as a human being with the animal's head. The god Horus is shown here with the head of a hawk. Gods could also be identified with symbols, for example Ma'at, the goddess of truth, was represented by a feather.

The huge columns in the Great Hypostyle Hall at the temple of Amun at Karnak

Temples

Gods were worshipped in temples and at home. Each village had a shrine where people could pray but there were also some enormous temples, such as the great temple of Amun at Karnak. Large numbers of priests led worship and organized important ceremonies and festivals connected with the gods.

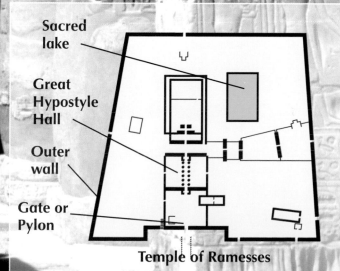

Sacred lake

Great Hypostyle Hall

Outer wall

Gate or Pylon

Temple of Ramesses

The Temple of Amun

This temple, like other large temples, was surrounded by a wall with a huge gateway, which we call a pylon. Only the priests and the king worshipped inside the temple, but during festivals the statues of the gods were paraded outside so that the people could worship them. The sacred lake was a place for the priests to purify themselves.

Gods and goddesses

There were hundreds of different gods and goddesses, and their importance and significance changed over time. Here are some of the most important.

Osiris

Ra

Ra was the sun god who created the world. He sailed across the sky every day in his boat and travelled through the underworld during the night, facing many dangers.

Osiris

Osiris was the god of the dead and ruler of the underworld, and is shown as a mummy wearing a crown. His kingdom was thought to be a perfect version of Egypt.

Isis

Isis was both the sister and wife of Osiris, and was the mother of Horus. She was associated with magic and was worshipped even outside Egypt.

Horus

The king was closely identified with Horus, but this god was popular with ordinary people too. Amulets, or lucky charms, of the 'eye of Horus' are often found and it is frequently shown in paintings. It was believed to bring protection and healing.

Eye of Horus

Hathor

A popular mother goddess, Hathor is often shown as a cow or as a woman with either a cow's head or just cow's ears. She was associated with the sky, but was also linked to other things, such as music and alcohol.

Amun

By the New Kingdom era, the local Theban god Amun had increased in importance and become ruler of the gods. He protected the king and the land of Egypt.

Anubis

Anubis, the god of cemeteries, is shown either as a jackal or as a human with a jackal's head. He was also the god of embalming, and he guided the dead through the underworld to the Afterlife.

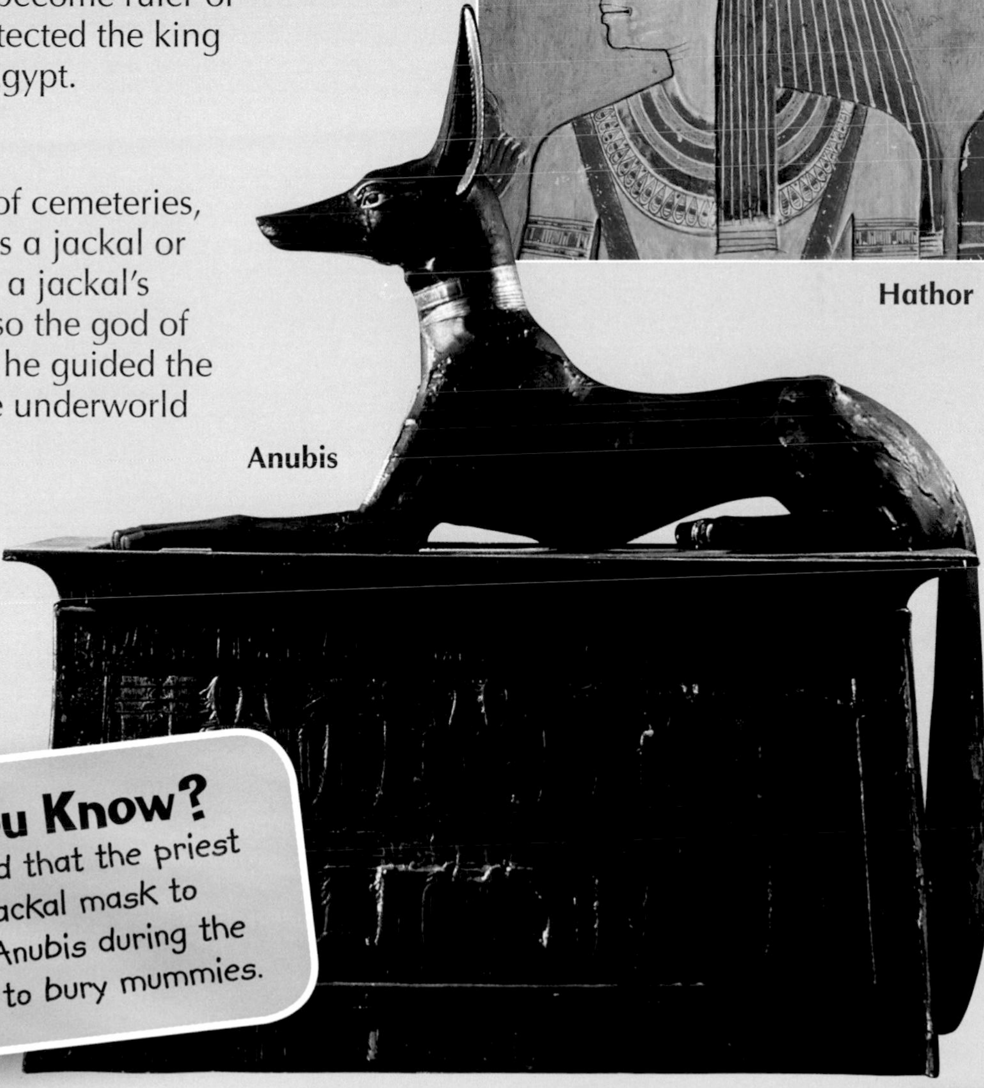

Anubis

Hathor

Did You Know?
It is believed that the priest wore a jackal mask to represent Anubis during the ceremonies to bury mummies.

The New Kingdom

The period called the New Kingdom lasted from about 1550 BC to 1069 BC. During this time Egypt was rich and powerful and many great monuments, which we can still see today, were built.

A massive sculpture of the pharaoh Ramesses II

A growing empire

During the New Kingdom, the amount of territory controlled by the Egyptian kings grew. Their empire stretched from Nubia in the south to beyond what is now Syria in the north. Taxes and trade from these new lands brought wealth to the Egyptian kings.

Giza
Memphis
Valley of the Kings
Thebes
The Nile
New Kingdom
Old Kingdom

Thebes

The New Kingdom's capital city was Thebes on the east bank of the Nile. Thebes became large and wealthy. The great Theban temple of Amun at Karnak became huge, as king after king added enormous columns, halls, scupltures and gateways.

The kings wanted to be buried near Thebes, too. They began preparing tombs in a dry valley in the mountains on the west bank of the Nile opposite the city. This became known as the Valley of the Kings.

The temple at Karnak

- The pharaoh Ramesses II ruled Egypt for around 66 years and is thought to have been over 90 years old when he died.

Temples of the kings

Kings hid their tombs in the Valley of the Kings but built splendid temples on the west bank of the Nile. Some were almost as big as the temples of the major gods. Here is the Ramesseum, the temple of the pharaoh Ramesses II.

Ruling the empire

The king was more than just a head of government – he was a god – but he needed help to govern Egypt.

This shield shows the pharaoh Tutankhamun as a sphinx wearing a crown, trampling on his enemies.

God king

In the beginning, Egyptians believed, the gods had ruled their land. When the gods left, the god Horus sent his spirit into the body of the king, and it passed to future rulers. Everything the king did was sacred, and rulers are always shown wearing a crown or holding special symbolic items.

Because the gods married their close relatives in Egyptian myths, kings frequently married their sisters or half-sisters. Sometimes they even married their daughters – though they had many other wives as well.

Administration

The king made all the important decisions which were then carried out by his officials. The king's most powerful adviser was called the vizier. The king was also helped by his ministers and the governors of the various provinces of Egypt. These officials often inherited their jobs, but an ambitious and intelligent scribe could always work his way up, as could a gifted soldier. Priests were important because of the wealth of their temples. They also collected taxes on behalf of the king.

Visiting nobles offer gifts to the pharaoh.

The army

During the New Kingdom the army became large and well organized, and Egyptian soldiers were feared in the surrounding countries. The army was made up of a mixture of foot soldiers and charioteers. The king always used a chariot. The soldiers came from many parts of the Egyptian Empire.

A dagger and sheath

A painting on a chest shows Tutankhamun in his chariot.

Queen Hatshepsut

Egypt was almost always ruled by men; the Egyptians thought that was how things had to be. But when the young ruler Tuthmosis II died, his successor was very unusual – it was his chief wife, Hatshepsut.

Hatshepsut

Hapshepsut had no sons but one of Tuthmosis II's other wives did. This boy was also called Tuthmosis, but he was too young to rule alone when his father died. From about 1479 BC Hatshepsut governed Egypt while the young heir grew up. Hatshepsut was a skilful ruler and after a few years she was declared to be the true 'king', ruling jointly with her stepson Tuthmosis III.

Hatshepsut is shown as a sphinx in this statue.

Did You Know?
After her death some of Hatshepsut's portraits and names were removed from monuments. There have been stories that Tuthmosis III hated his stepmother and it was he who had her name removed. They actually seem to have ruled well together, with Tuthmosis away leading the army and Hatshepsut governing at home.

In search of treasures

During Hatshepsut's reign an expedition went to the land of Punt (perhaps Somalia), and details are recorded on her temple's walls. Traders brought back precious goods including leopard skins, ivory and even live baboons.

Queen Hatshepsut built a beautiful temple at Deir el-Bahri. Originally it would have had trees and flowerbeds around it.

The royal beard

The false beard worn by Egyptian kings is a symbol of royalty; even Hatshepsut is sometimes shown with one. In this statue only a small part of the beard remains. Experts are not certain whether this is a sculpture of Hatshepsut or of her husband Tuthmosis II.

The Valley of the Kings

On the west bank of the Nile opposite Thebes are mountains and great cliffs. Cutting into them are deep valleys, ideal for hiding royal tombs dug into the rocks.

The valley

The valley where the kings chose to build their tombs had few entrances and no villages nearby. It could easily be guarded. The rough cliffs meant that the entrances to royal tombs, with their precious contents, could be hidden. However, only one tomb survived almost complete – the boy king Tutankhamun's.

Some nobles and courtiers were buried in the Valley of the Kings as well, but most had their tombs cut from the rock in places close to the Valley of the Kings. Later in the New Kingdom, queens were buried in a nearby valley, now called the Valley of the Queens.

Top Facts

- The burial sites in the valley have all been given numbers by the archaeologists. One tomb, called KV5, is huge, with more than 150 rooms and corridors. It is only partly explored.

- One of the most beautifully decorated of the royal tombs is that of Nefertari, which is in the Valley of the Queens.

Did You Know?

Many of the tombs were robbed soon after the kings had been buried and the doors sealed. The thieves were probably the same people who built or filled them. Selling the precious contents could bring in a lot of money but was very risky. Anyone who was caught faced a horrible death: being impaled on a sharp stake.

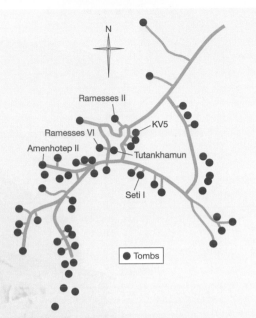

So far more than 60 burial sites have been discovered in the Valley of the Kings.

Map labels: Ramesses II, KV5, Ramesses VI, Amenhotep II, Tutankhamun, Seti I, N, ● Tombs

Treasure

The jewel box of Tutankhamun's great-grandmother, Thuya, was found in the Valley of the Kings in 1905. She and her husband had been buried there even though they were not members of the royal family because their daughter, Tiye, had married King Amenhotep III.

The tombs

The royal tombs vary in size and shape, but all have steep corridors and steps leading down into the ground. Most were beautifully decorated by the best artists in the country, many of whom lived some hours' walk away.

Many tombs are unfinished as it took a long time to dig them out of the rock. The only tools were made of stone, wood and the soft metals copper and bronze. Once out of daylight workers used oil lamps in the narrow spaces. Working conditions must have been cramped and unpleasant. This picture shows the tourist entrance of the tomb of the pharaoh Ramesses VI in the Valley of the Kings.

Tutankhamun's tomb

The boy king Tutankhamun was almost forgotten until the British Egyptologist Howard Carter made a discovery that astonished the world.

The sealed door

In 1915 a wealthy man called Lord Carnarvon had employed Howard Carter to look for a royal tomb in the Valley of the Kings. Carter found nothing of importance until, on 4 November 1922, his diggers cleared some huts away and saw steps. They led down to a sealed door and Tutankhamun's name was written on the door.

The mask

The famous mask from the king's mummy is made from sheet gold, precious stones and glass. It weighs nearly 10.5 kilograms.

Wonderful things

On 25 November 1922, Lord Carnarvon stood behind Carter as the archaeologist peered through a hole in another blocked door. "What can you see?" asked Carnarvon. "Wonderful things!" Carter answered.

Nobody had seen inside the tomb for over 3000 years – and it was full of objects. Gold glittered everywhere they looked.

The tomb

The four small rooms of Tutankhamun's tomb were packed with treasures.

Annexe

3rd door

Antechamber

Burial chamber

2nd door

Passage

Treasury

1st Door

The curse of Tutankhamun

Lord Carnarvon died after being bitten by a mosquito shortly after the tomb was discovered and tales of an Ancient Egyptian curse began to spread. There is no evidence of one, though. Most of the other people involved lived long lives. Howard Carter, shown here examining Tutankhamun's coffin, died in 1939, 15 years after he first entered the tomb.

Ancient treasures

Clearing the four-roomed tomb took many years. It contained jewellery, such as the beetle-shaped jewel shown here, beds, thrones, statues, fans, chariots and food and wine for the Afterlife. There were also weapons, trumpets, games and even a lock of hair from Tutankhamun's grandmother, Queen Tiye. There was also the body, and the solid gold coffin, of the king himself.

Tutankhamun – the golden king

The best-known king of Egypt ruled for only a short time. Little is known about his reign, but his name lives on because of the discovery of his tomb.

The boy king

Tutankhamun was 8 or 9 years old when he came to the throne. He was married to one of his half-sisters, Ankhesenamun. Tutankhamun and his young wife are shown on many of the treasures found in his tomb, such as this beautiful golden throne.

This wooden statue of Tutankhamun may have been used to make sure new clothes fitted him.

Advisers

All Egyptian kings had advisers, but Tutankhamun's advisers ruled Egypt for him because he was so young. Tutankhamun would have taken part in religious ceremonies. Ay (shown above on the right) was the most important member of Tutankhamun's court and had a great deal of power. Ay became king after Tutankhamun's death. Horemheb was another adviser. He commanded the army, and ruled Egypt after Ay.

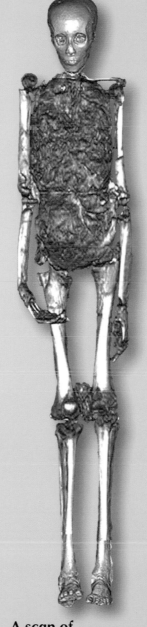

A scan of Tutankhamun's body

Top Facts

- Tutankhamun died in the month of January. Scientists can tell this from the types of flowers found in his tomb.

- Tutankhamun and Ankhesenamun had no living children, but the mummified bodies of two premature babies were found in his tomb.

Death of a young king

Tutankhamun died suddenly in about 1327 BC, aged 19 or 20. Some archaeologists thought he was murdered, but a recent scan of his body showed damage to one leg, which may have happened before he died. He could have been injured, possibly in a chariot accident, and the wound might have become infected. Murder now looks unlikely, but we still don't know exactly how he died.

Scribes

The Ancient Egyptians kept written records, but most people could not read or write. A scribe who was able to do both could become quite wealthy.

Scribes

There was always work for scribes – writing letters, records or contracts. The government relied on scribes, and an intelligent man could become a royal adviser. A scribe might also become involved in other work, such as engineering or surveying.

Most important organizations, such as the army or the temples, trained their own scribes. Most trainees were the sons of scribes, and boys began training between the ages of 5 and 10. Girls were not usually taught to write.

Top facts

- In Egyptian art, scribes were shown sitting cross-legged with a papyrus scroll on their knees.

- Black ink was often made from a mixture of soot, gum and water. Red ink was made from red clay.

Papyrus

Papyrus was the first paper in the world. It was made from the pith, the inner part of the stem, of papyrus reeds that grew along the banks of the River Nile. During the time of the Ancient Egyptians, hippopotamuses lived along the Nile, so collecting the reeds could be a dangerous job! Ink was black or red and came dry in a small block, which was moistened with a little water. Pens were made from reeds.

Did You Know?
The inside of the papyrus stem was used to produce paper, but the coarser outer layer of the stem was used in making baskets and ropes and even in boat-building.

Ostraca

Papyrus was too expensive to use for writing practice and so pieces of scrap pottery, called ostraca, were given to trainee scribes. This pottery could be washed and used many times. Wooden tablets or pieces of limestone were used instead of papyrus for less important documents.

A scribe's ink palette and reed pens. Palettes were often made from limestone.

Hieroglyphics

The main Egyptian form of writing, called hieroglyphics, was a system of more than 700 picture symbols. The Egyptians thought they had been given the gift of writing by Thoth, the god of wisdom. They believed that the picture symbols used in their hieroglyphics had a magic power.

How do hieroglyphics work?

Hieroglyphics are seen on monuments and in tomb paintings. They are often beautifully carved or drawn but can be very difficult to understand. Hieroglyphics can be written in any direction – from left to right, from right to left or from top to bottom. Bird symbols always face the start of a sentence, so readers can tell which way it runs. Bands of hieroglyphics are separated by lines. The individual pictures can sometimes represent things, such as a goose or a man. Sometimes they stand for sounds.

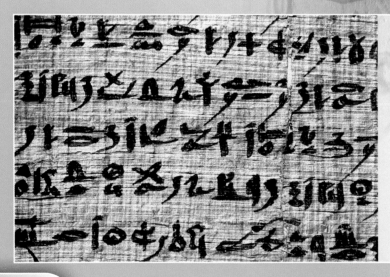

Simpler ways of writing

Hieroglyphics were difficult to use and a simpler form of writing, called hieratic, developed. You can see an example of hieractic writing on papyrus here. Eventually another even quicker method of writing was invented. This was called demotic, but hieroglyphics continued to be used.

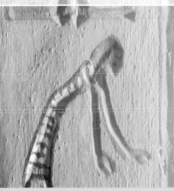

The Rosetta Stone

Nobody could read hieroglyphics when the Rosetta Stone was found in Egypt in 1799. The same text appears in three places on the stone – written in hieroglyphics at the top, then demotic and Greek at the bottom. Scholars understood Greek, so in 1822, Jean-François Champollion, an expert in languages, was able to use the Greek to work out what the other two languages said.

Hieroglyphic writing

Demotic writing

Greek writing

Tutankhamun's cartouche

Top Facts

- There were no hieroglyphic symbols for vowels, so Egyptologists have to guess what they might be.
- The inscription on the Rosetta Stone records religious ceremonies held during the coronation of King Ptolemy V in 205 BC.

Kings' names

Kings' names are easily recognized. They are always in an oval frame called a cartouche. The one on the left of this fan is the cartouche of Tutankhamun.

Working life

Ancient Egyptian people worked hard, from important officials in the royal court to poor slaves in the quarries.

Merchants and traders

Egypt traded grain, wine, linen and precious goods such as gold with other countries. In return merchants brought oil, wood, silver, copper, horses and even slaves into the country.

The Nile was the main way of transporting goods and many ordinary Egyptians worked on the boats, which had oars as well as sails. Heavy loads were carried by large barges towed by many other boats. There were fishermen on the river, too.

Did You Know?

Traders explored the lands around Egypt in search of rare goods. They often crossed the eastern desert to the Red Sea. The traders' ships were taken apart and carried across the desert to the coast, where they were rebuilt so they could continue their voyage.

Did You Know?

Egyptians didn't use money, but paid for things they wanted in goods or work they could do.

Making things

There were many skilled people including carpenters, jewellers, weavers and potters. The men shown here are making jewellery. Some worked in workshops, supervised by overseers. These overseers were in charge of security when the workers were using valuable materials.

Many other things were also made. Beer was brewed, bread baked, reeds were cut and made into papyrus for scribes to write on and mud bricks were made for buildings. People worked for the embalmers and there were entertainers, servants and slaves, too.

Top Facts

- Richer Egyptians had servants to help them in their homes. Slaves were not common until the New Kingdom when many prisoners of war were captured, and even ordinary Egyptians could use these captives as slaves.

- Scribes kept workshop records, so we know that one craftsman had a day off because he had drunk too much beer.

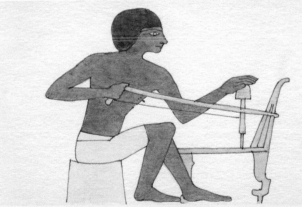

Carpenters

Carpenters produced furniture such as beds, stools and chests as well as games and toys for the home. This man is making a chair. Wood was also used to make larger objects. The large barges used to carry goods on the Nile were usually built from cedar wood, and chariots were mainly constructed from timber. Carpenters mainly used local soft timbers such as sycamore but imported hardwoods such as cedar and ebony were valued for their strength and beauty.

Women and children

Women generally did not go out to work but they had many of the same rights as men, and daughters were as important as sons.

Getting married

Kings could marry several wives, but most ordinary men had only one and married when they were about 20 years old. Women were often younger. People's partners were usually chosen by their parents, but there is evidence that they often loved each other, too. Most people got married.

The majority of women probably couldn't read or write, but they could own property or run businesses, particularly if their husbands were away. Wealthy women were better educated, and could become priestesses. Others might find work as entertainers or servants, and some were weavers or ran farms.

Top Facts

- **Women such as Cleopatra could become rulers of the country, and queens were often powerful.**

- **Lessons in school were strict. Boys were beaten if they behaved badly.**

The pharaoh Akhenaten and his most famous wife Nefertiti

Being young

Egyptian children played with dolls, balls, board games and pull-along animals on wheels – very much like the kinds of toys we have today. They also enjoyed swimming, fishing and riding donkeys. This game (above) involving a die was found in the Temple of Bes at Bawiti in the west of Egypt.

Unlike today, not all children went to school; it depended on whether their parents could afford to send them. Those who weren't educated were sent out to work or helped in family businesses as soon as they were able to do so.

A painting from the tomb of Inherka shows a family scene.

Clothing and jewellery

Fashions didn't change much in Ancient Egypt and most clothing was simple. Rich people often dressed more lavishly, and everyone liked jewellery.

Getting dressed

Most clothes were made of linen. Wealthy people wore fine cloth and poorer people wore thicker, more hard-wearing fabric. Men wore a kilt and women a full-length dress with shoulder straps. In the New Kingdom, fine-pleated linen became fashionable, and some men and women wore overgarments of almost transparent material.

Most people went barefoot but some sandals, made of reeds, have survived. People either shaved their heads or had short hair but they often wore wigs, which could be elaborate.

Top Facts

- Both men and women wore dark eye make-up made of minerals mixed with water.

- Boys shaved their heads except for a lock of hair on one side, which was allowed to grow. This was called the sidelock of youth.

These people are dressed in their best clothes. They are in the Afterlife, worshipping the green-faced gods of the underworld.

Perfume cone

a collar made from gold and precious stones

Jewellery

Everyone wore some jewellery, such as necklaces with good-luck charms on them. Bracelets were popular, and so were rings and earrings. Rich people owned many luxurious pieces. Big 'collars' were worn by both men and women. They were made of many strings of beads or precious stones and formed a semi-circle around the neck and over the top of the chest.

Nefertiti, wife of the pharaoh Akhenaten, is wearing a jewelled collar in this statue.

Feasts and festivals

We know from tomb paintings how much people enjoyed having a good time. They wanted this to continue in the Afterlife.

Throwing parties

There were public festivals, such as the huge processions of the statue of the god Amun around Thebes, but also private parties where people entertained their friends. At these parties there was plenty of food and drink, and guests were welcomed with garlands of flowers. They sat on stools and were waited upon by servants as they listened to musicians and watched dancers.

Top Facts

- Entertainers, including acrobats and dancing girls, were hired for parties.
- There was a list of days that were supposed to be either lucky or unlucky. On unlucky days you weren't allowed to eat certain types of food, such as fish.

What was served?

Those who could afford it drank wine – beer was a cheaper alternative. There was also plenty of cooked meat and fresh vegetables. Local fruits such as pomegranates, figs and dates were piled high.

Women offer each other lotus flowers at a feast.

Music

During a party musicians played harps and lyres as well as wind instruments such as pipes and flutes. There might also have been percussion instruments such as cymbals, drums and tambourines. Some musicians played solos but groups of musicians seem to have been more usual.

A banquet scene from the tomb of the nobleman Nebamun

Fun and games

Hunting was one of the ways the rich enjoyed themselves, but all Ancient Egyptians played games and some of their board games and toys have survived.

The hunt

The king and his courtiers went hunting in the deserts where there were wild animals such as gazelles and antelopes. There were wild bulls and lions, too. The king was safe, though – he hunted from a chariot.

Dangerous river animals such as hippos and crocodiles were hunted to protect people who worked near the river. Birds such as wild ducks, which nested in the reed thickets, were hunted from boats. Birds were brought down using a curved throwing stick like the the one being used by the man in the wall painting below.

Top Facts

- When the king went hunting the animals were rounded up so that he could shoot arrows at them one by one.
- Children's balls were made of cloth or leather and were stuffed with straw, horsehair or thread.

A wall painting shows a cat helping on a duck hunt.

62

Games

Board games were very popular and one – senet – even developed a religious meaning as a battle between good and evil. A senet board was divided into 30 squares, but nobody knows exactly how it was played.

There were other games, such as the 'game of snake' or the 'game of twenty squares'. These also involved moving pieces around a board divided into sections.

Playing ball games was common, and complicated throwing and catching games seem to have been popular with girls.

A senet board

Did You Know?

When a nobleman went to hunt birds in the marshes he might take his wife. He would definitely need his servants – and he would also take along his cat to help!

An Egyptian joke

The game of senet wasn't always taken seriously. In this picture, painted on papyrus, an antelope and a lion are shown playing against each other.

The end of Ancient Egypt

With the death of Ramesses XI in 1070 BC, the New Kingdom came to an end. Gradually Egypt's power faded until, in about 31 BC, it became part of the Roman Empire.

Invasions

There were many different invasions in the last 1000 years BC. There were Libyan, Nubian and Assyrian rulers, and then the Persians conquered the land. The Egyptians rebelled but the Persians returned.

Top Facts

- Cleopatra wasn't actually Egyptian. She was a descendant of Ptolemy, a Greek.
- Cleopatra married her younger brother, Ptolemy XIII, so that she could claim the throne of Egypt. A woman could usually only inherit if she married a close male relative.

This Victorian painting shows Octavian's fleet surrounding Mark Antony's ships at the Battle of Actium.

Alexander the Great

The Persians were finally thrown out of Egypt by the Greek king, Alexander the Great, in 332 BC. Alexander died less than ten years later and his empire was split into three parts. One of his generals, Ptolemy, took control of Egypt. Ptolemy's descendants ruled for nearly 300 years.

Roman influence

A new state developed in the Mediterranean in about 150–100 BC. It was called Rome. The Ptolemies remained kings of Egypt, but had to tolerate Roman influence.

Did You Know?

Both Antony and Cleopatra killed themselves after their defeat. Antony stabbed himself and Cleopatra is supposed to have poisoned herself with a snake, but it could have been a poisoned comb or hairpin. There were just two tiny scratches on her arm.

Cleopatra

In 51 BC Cleopatra VII became queen of Egypt. A civil war began almost immediately and the Roman general Julius Caesar arrived to defend Cleopatra.

After Julius Caesar's death in 44 BC, Cleopatra made an alliance with Caesar's friend Mark Antony. Julius Caesar's Roman heir, Octavian, didn't want any rivals for power and war broke out between Rome and Antony and Cleopatra. Antony and Cleopatra were defeated at the Battle of Actium in 31 BC and Egypt became part of the Roman Empire.

ANCIENT GREECE

Ancient Greece was not one country but was made up of a number of independent states. Each had its own laws and currency. The city states, which became powerful from about 800 BC, spoke the same language and had the same religion but they frequently fought one another. Many ideas that are still important today originated in these cities – Athens gave us the basis of our modern form of government, democracy. Many of the activities that we enjoy today such as storytelling, theatre and sporting competition were as important to the Ancient Greeks as they are to us.

The Minoans

Crete is the largest of the Greek islands and was home to a great civilization which flourished between 2500 BC and 1450 BC. Nobody really knew much about this civilization until the archaeologist Arthur Evans discovered an enormous palace at Knossos in 1900. He called the people who lived there the Minoans, after the legendary Cretan king Minos.

Learning from Minoan art

Minoan palaces had beautiful wall paintings and some have been found in ordinary homes, too. These paintings tell us a lot about life at the time. Waves and sea creatures such as dolphins were often shown in wall paintings, reflecting the importance of the sea in the Minoans' lives. We have also learned what the Minoans looked like from these pictures.

A wall painting from the palace of Knossos shows two young men wearing kilts.

Top Facts

- **People lived on the upper floors of houses, and used the downstairs for cooking or storage.**

- **Objects made by the Minoans have been found all over the eastern Mediterranean and must have been traded by Minoan sailors.**

Did You Know?

Plenty of written records have been found on Crete — but we can't read them. The main form of writing is known as Linear A, and nobody has been able to understand it.

Minoan religion

Bulls also often appear in paintings or on pots, and bulls' horns were used to decorate walls and tombs. This bull's head (right), called a rhyton, was used during religious ceremonies. It contained liquids, which were offered to the gods. The Minoans worshipped their gods in small shrines or in the countryside. Female priests are often shown in their paintings, and they may have been more important than male priests.

Pot in the shape of a bull's head

69

The palace of Knossos

When Arthur Evans began to explore the palace of Knossos, he realized that the building was so complicated that it could be described as a labyrinth or maze. He thought the palace might have been the labyrinth described in the Greek story of Theseus and the Minotaur.

The palace of Knossos

Knossos was the largest palace in Crete, and as many as 30,000 people may have lived there. It was built mostly of stone, with wooden ceilings and roofs. In places it was several storeys high. There were rooms, courtyards, staircases and lots of corridors. There were huge storerooms for food and workshops for craftsmen.

We don't know who ruled Knossos, but there was a room that looks like a throne room, in which there is a seat made of stone built against the wall.

The grand staircase

- Parts of the palace of Knossos were restored by Arthur Evans so visitors today can see what it might have looked like originally.

- Three other palaces have been found on Crete but Knossos is the largest.

The remains of the palace of Knossos covers about 25,000 square metres.

The story of the Minotaur

The myths tell that Theseus, a prince from Athens, sailed to Crete, where he was forced to fight a terrible creature called the Minotaur. The Minotaur was half man, half bull, and was kept in the Labyrinth – a building like a maze – by King Minos, the ruler of Crete.

The king's daughter, Ariadne, fell in love with Theseus. Before he entered the Labyrinth to fight the Minotaur, Ariadne gave him a ball of thread which he unwound as he went into the Labyrinth so that he could find his way back by following it. Theseus killed the Minotaur, then he and Ariadne fled from Crete, escaping her angry father.

The end of the Minoan world

In about 1450 BC, the Minoan way of life died out quite mysteriously and no one really knows why. Many archaeologists think that a natural disaster may have been partly to blame.

Top Facts

- Volcanic ash lying deep over fields would have made it almost impossible to grow food or raise animals.

- Large blocks of stone have been ripped out of position at Amnisos on Crete, probably by a huge tidal wave.

Natural disasters

The island of Thera was a volcano, and it was only about 100 kilometres from Crete. In about 1450 BC there was a a massive eruption. Thera was blown apart (parts survived and these are now called Santorini). The eruption would have triggered earthquakes and tidal waves, causing many deaths and damage to buildings and farms, even in Crete.

Did You Know?

Hundreds of years after the Minoans lived, the Greek philosopher Plato wrote that there was once a powerful kingdom called Atlantis. He said it was an island and had sunk beneath the sea. Some people think that Minoan Crete may be the original Atlantis.

Fires and invaders

What happened after the eruption is uncertain. Some people came back to the palaces for a while, but in about 1350 BC most of the palaces were destroyed by fire. It looks as though Crete was invaded by Mycenaeans – people from the Greek mainland. Knossos was rebuilt, but it burnt down again in about 1100 BC. This time it was abandoned.

The remains of Akrotiri

Akrotiri – the lost village

A Minoan village called Akrotiri was discovered on the island of Santorini in the 1960s. Akrotiri had been buried in volcanic ash, but its people seem to have escaped. Streets and houses survive, as do many beautiful paintings of everyday life such as the fisherboy above. Few precious items have been found – their owners probably took those with them when they fled.

The Mycenaeans

The warlike Mycenaeans were another powerful Bronze Age people. They took their name from the city of Mycenae.

Mycenaea

Mycenaea seems to have been made up from several small kingdoms rather than one large one. Mycenae itself was probably the biggest city. Like the others, it was built on a hill. It would have been easy to defend. Inside its enormous walls were the palace and many other buildings such as shrines, workshops and the tombs of some previous rulers. It had a huge gateway guarded by the figures of two lions, which was probably built in about 1250 BC.

The Lion Gateway

Mycenaean writing

Mycenaean writing is similar to Minoan, and is called Linear B. We can understand it but, so far, mainly just lists of goods and officials have been found.

Mycenaean graves

There are huge beehive-shaped tombs at Mycenae. These stone buildings were constructed in about 1500 BC. The city's rulers would have been buried here when they died, with elaborate ceremonies and valuable possessions. None of the treasures have been found because all of these tombs were robbed a long time ago.

Earlier kings were buried in shaft graves – deep holes in the ground that were not so easy to rob. In 1876, the archaeologist Heinrich Schliemann opened the graves. He found five gold death masks as well as other precious things in gold, silver and bronze, such as jewellery and cups.

Top Facts

- The ruins at Mycenae were so vast that people once thought they had been built by giants.

- By about 1200 BC the Mycenaean world was coming to an end and the cities were abandoned.

Agamemnon

According to myths and legends the king of Mycenae during the Trojan War was called Agamemnon. When Heinrich Schliemann found the gold death masks, he called one the 'mask of Agamemnon'. However, the mask dates from about 1550 BC, which is about 250 years before the time of the Trojan War.

The Trojan War

The story of *The Iliad* by the Greek poet Homer tells of the Trojan War, between the Greek leaders and the king of Troy – a city in what is now Turkey. This story was thought to be a legend until archaeological evidence began to appear.

Homer's story

Helen, Queen of the Greek city of Sparta, ran away with Paris, a prince from Troy. Her husband Menelaus and his brother Agamemnon organized a great army to get her back. The Greek army besieged the city of Troy for ten years but, eventually, the Greeks pretended to leave. They left behind a huge wooden horse that the people of Troy, the Trojans, took into the city, believing that it was a gift for the goddess Athene. They did not realize that Greek soldiers had hidden inside the horse. At night the Greeks climbed out and opened the gates to let in their army so that the city of Troy was captured.

Top Facts

- Visitors to Troy today can climb inside a giant wooden horse.

- When Homer wrote his great poems, *The Iliad* and *The Odyssey*, in about 800 BC, he was writing down stories people had been telling for hundreds of years.

The discovery of Troy

Most people thought that Troy did not really exist until the archaeologist Heinrich Schliemann began to dig at Hissarlik in Turkey in the 1870s and found the remains of a series of cities, one on top of the other. They were just where Homer had said Troy was. Some of these cities had been destroyed by force and one of them is likely to be Homer's Troy. However, any war between the Greeks and the Trojans was probably about trade and land rather than a woman.

Treasure

Heinrich Schliemann found treasures, such as golden jewellery and cups, in the ruins of Troy. Archaeologists think that these objects are too old to have had anything to do with the Trojan War.

Illustration of the soldiers leaving the wooden horse

The growth of the city states

The period in Greek history between 800 BC and 500 BC is known as the Archaic Period. Cities such as Athens, Sparta and Corinth had become more important than other towns. These large cities controlled the countryside around them, forming city states.

Some of the remains of Corinth, one of the more important city states.

City states

Each city state was independent. They were often ruled by councils, not usually by kings, and had their own armies. Athens, Sparta and Corinth were the strongest city states, but there were also smaller ones.

The city states sometimes fought each other, but they had strong links, too. Their people all spoke Greek and had the same religion, though they had their own laws and ways of governing.

Did You Know?

Sparta was ruled by a council of 30 — two Kings and 28 men over the age of 60. They made all the decisions. It also had an assembly of 60 members but the members weren't allowed to discuss decisions — they could only vote for or against them. They did this by yelling either 'yes!' or 'no!'. The side which could shout the loudest won.

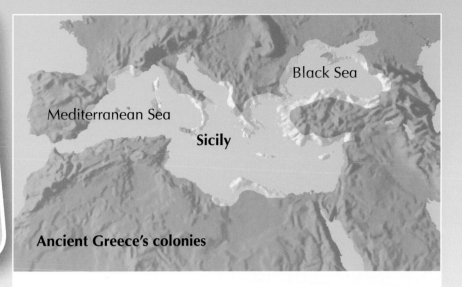

Ancient Greece's colonies

Black Sea

Mediterranean Sea

Sicily

Expansion

From about 1000 bc people began to leave the Greek mainland. They formed colonies abroad, and these became states. Many were on the shores of the Black Sea, but they were also in Egypt, Sicily, southern Italy and France. Some became very wealthy. The colonies were important. Most Greek city states could not grow enough food, for example, and grain often had to be brought in from the settlements around the Black Sea.

The Greeks in Sicily

A number of city states founded colonies on Sicily. The Corinthians settled at Syracuse, which became the largest of the Greek towns on the island. Here (left) we can see the remains of the theatre at Syracuse.

Sparta

The city of Sparta in southern Greece became one of the largest and most powerful of the city states. But living there could be hard because all of life in Sparta centred around building a strong army.

A military state

Every Spartan citizen had to become a soldier. Their entire lives were spent training and learning about war. They ate and slept in barracks and did not often go home, even when they married. Citizens were men (no women) who had been born there, never outsiders. Men who were not citizens were either *perioikoi* or *helots*. The first were free men who could trade and serve in the army. Helots did all the work on the land and were almost slaves, even though they were living in the area before the army took over.

Spartan soldiers wore scarlet cloaks and often had long hair.

Did You Know?

Spartan girls did sport like boys, which the other Greek states thought very odd.

Spartan women

Women could not become full citizens of Sparta. They were trained to ensure they were fit and would have strong babies who could become powerful warriors. Spartan women were supposed to be as tough as the men.

The Krater of Vix

This giant container, found in a chieftan's grave in France, was made by Spartan craftsmen, who were not citizens. The pot is over 1.5 metres tall and the rim is decorated with pictures of Greek warriors. Spartan craftsmen were famous for the beauty of their metalwork, but as the city increasingly concentrated on building its army, interest in the arts and crafts decreased.

The remains of Sparta today

Did You Know?

New babies were examined by officials. If they looked ill, weak or generally unlikely to grow into promising adults, they would be left outside the city to die.

Fighting on land and sea

The Greek city states were frequently at war, both with each other and with invaders such as the Persians. Greek armies were well trained and successful, and their navies were strong, too.

Ships

The most powerful Greek warships were called triremes, large ships with three ranks of oars. These were fast and easy to steer, and had bronze battering rams on the front to damage other ships. Triremes were very expensive both to build and to crew, so only the richest states could afford them.

Soldiers on horseback

At first, soldiers on horseback or riding in chariots were the most important in Greek armies. As they had to provide their own horses and equipment, only wealthy people could fight in this way.

The Greeks used many different ships, not just big triremes. Like this one, triremes were powered by oars but they had sails as well.

Top Facts

- Each hoplite could decide how to decorate his round shield.

- Triremes were stored in ship sheds close to the port during the winter when the sea was too rough to sail them.

Hoplites

By the seventh century BC foot soldiers, called hoplites, formed the main force in all the Greek armies. The hoplites were well armoured with bronze chest and back plates, leg guards and helmets. They had bronze and leather shields and mainly used long spears but also had iron swords. Athenian soliders used a formation known as a phalanx – a long line of soldiers four or eight rows deep. Generals would always try to attack enemy phalanxes on the right, as the men there were always more exposed.

Did You Know?

Only the richest soldiers could afford armour and spears. Poorer soldiers used slingshots and stones, or bows and arrows.

83

The Persian Wars

In the sixth century BC Greek city states were under threat from Persia – a huge and powerful country that is now called Iran.

Trouble begins

In 546 BC the Persians took over the Greek territories in Ionia (now western Turkey). The Ionian people rebelled in 500–449 BC, but were defeated. The city of Athens had helped the Ionians so the Persian king, Darius, decided to punish it.

The battle at Marathon

Darius landed his army at Marathon, quite close to Athens. The Athenians, together with their allies, formed an army and won an astonishing victory against the much larger Persian forces.

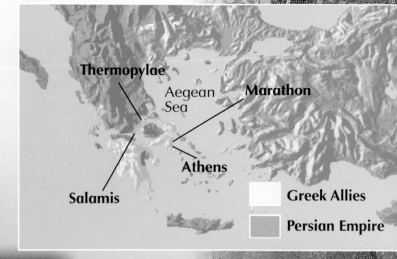

Thermopylae

Aegean Sea

Marathon

Athens

Salamis

Greek Allies

Persian Empire

The Persian king Darius in his chariot

Persian revenge

The next Persian king, Xerxes, invaded Greece again in 480 BC. His vast army first met the Greeks at a narrow pass, Thermopylae. Today, a statue of the Spartan king Leonidas commemorates the Greek soldiers who died at the pass while trying to hold back the Persian army. The Greeks were defeated and the Persians marched down to Athens.

Did You Know?

After the victory at Marathon, a messenger was sent to Athens. He ran the 37 kilometres (26 miles), delivered the news, then dropped dead from exhaustion. Modern marathon races take their name from this feat.

The defeat of Persia at Salamis

The Athenians' best chance of defeating Xerxes' Persian army was in a sea battle, as the Athenian ships were much better. In 480 BC the Persian navy was lured into a trap at Salamis and was almost destroyed. This Greek victory was followed by one on land at Plataea and another at sea – and by 479 BC the Persian occupation was over.

After the final Persian defeat, the Greek city states vowed to defend each other in the future.

Athens

Athens was named after Athene, the goddess of wisdom and war. It was the biggest city in Greece and one of the most powerful city states. Some of the ideas of the people of Ancient Athens are still important today.

The growth of Athens

The years from 500 to 336 BC are known as the Classical Period and during this time the city of Athens flourished. In 449 BC Pericles, the popular Athenian politician and army general, began work on rebuilding the temples on the Acropolis, which had been damaged during the Persian Wars. Athens became a centre for trade, culture and learning, including science, medicine and philosophy.

Did You Know?
Athens was enormous during the Classical period. There may have been almost 250,000 people living there.

The Acropolis of Athens

Did You Know?
There were laws in Athens — but no lawyers. Instead citizens had to do jury service, judging cases. Each jury had more than 200 men, which made it impossible for all of them to be threatened or bribed.

Living in the city

The highest part of Athens was a hill called the Acropolis, where the main temples were. People lived and worked on the flat land below the Acropolis. The most important area in a Greek town was the *agora*, a large market place. Around it were *stoas* (left), long buildings with shops where people could meet. Craftsmen's workshops have been found near the *agora* in Athens.

Silver coin

Wealth

Athens was inland, but had a port called Piraeus on the coast nearby. The port was vital for trade, which brought money to the city. The silver mines at Laurion, near the city, were also a source of wealth for Athens. Thousands of slaves worked in these mines. Athenian coins were made from the silver.

Democracy

An Athenian called Cleisthenes set up an Assembly where every citizen could be heard and have a vote. This system of ruling was called democracy, which comes from the Greek words *demos*, meaning 'people', and *kratos*, meaning 'rule'. Women, slaves and foreigners, however, were not citizens. This system of governing by giving each citizen a vote is used by many countries today.

The Acropolis and the Parthenon

The most famous of all Ancient Greek buildings is the Parthenon. It was the largest temple on the Acropolis and stands on the highest point on the hill.

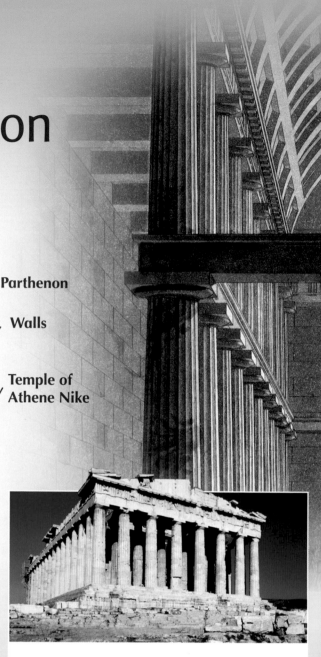

Parthenon

Walls

Temple of Athene Nike

The Acropolis

The main temple on the Acropolis was the Parthenon but there were other important temples on there, too, for example the temple of Athene Nike – the victorious Athene – which was decorated with carvings of the Trojan War. The temples were surrounded by a strong wall with a large gateway.

The Parthenon

The Parthenon belonged to the goddess Athene and was used a bit like a treasury, storing many gold and silver offerings to her. The building was undamaged for 2000 years until, in 1687, gunpowder stored there exploded and the centre of the temple was destroyed.

This illustration dating from the 1900s gives an impression of what the Parthenon may have looked like inside.

Top Facts

- The Parthenon was once covered in sculptures. Many were removed and sold to the British Museum in London at the beginning of the 1800s.

- The great statue of Athene in the Parthenon is supposed to have cost more than the building itself. It was made by Pheidias, a friend of the Athenian leader Pericles.

Did You Know?

Just inside the Parthenon was a huge statue of the goddess Athene. It was nearly 12 metres high and made from wood and ivory. The statue wore clothes made from gold, which were taken off if there was any danger that the statue might be stolen by invaders.

Greek columns

Many Greek buildings, such as the Parthenon, have columns which look as though they are the same width all the way up, but they're not. When you look up at a column that is straight, it seems thinner in the middle. The architects wanted their columns to look perfectly straight – so they made them fatter in the middle.

The Peloponnesian Wars

A sculpture of a foot soldier

A struggle for power between Athens and Sparta began in 431 BC. Athens was supported by its colonies and Sparta made alliances with its neighbouring states in the Peloponnes, an area in southern Greece. The wars that followed are called the Peloponnesian Wars and they lasted for more than 20 years.

Athens and Sparta

As Athens grew richer and more powerful, some of the smaller city states felt threatened. The nobles who ruled Sparta were particularly worried about the Athenian idea of democracy which would have destroyed their control of the state.

In 460 BC Athens built the Long Walls linking the city to the port of Piraeus. This meant that traders were always able to reach the sea and its powerful navy, even if Athens was besieged. Sparta thought that Athens had done this because it was preparing for war.

Athens extended its walls down to the port of Piraeus.

War

In 435 BC, fighting started between the state of Corinth and its colony Corfu. Athens and Sparta took different sides. Sparta declared war on Athens and its army marched towards the city in 431 BC. Athens could hold out against a siege because food could be brought in through the port of Piraeus, but disease spread in the city, killing a huge number of people. In the end a truce was signed in 421 BC and the first Peloponnesian war ended.

Disaster for Athens

War broke out again, and in 415 BC the Athenians lost nearly 200 ships following a betrayal. Athens became weaker as its allies began to desert it and Sparta grew stronger by forming an alliance with Persia. Athens was attacked and besieged again. It had to surrender in 404 BC, ending the second Peloponnesian War.

Macedonia rises

Most people in the Greek city states thought the people of Macedonia in the north-east of Greece were barbarians. They never imagined that Macedonia would become a great power.

Macedonia
in 359 BC
in 336 BC

THRACE

MACEDONIA

GREECE

Macedonia and King Philip

Macedonia had a violent history of wars and invasions. When Philip II became Macedonia's ruler in 359 BC he restored order to the kingdom. He then started looking outside its borders for places to conquer.

Conquests

Philip took control of Thessaly and Thrace, adding huge areas of territory to Macedonia. This made the city states, such as Athens and Thebes, nervous and they joined together against him. Philip won a victory over them in 338 BC at Chaeronea. He planned to attack Persia next.

A sculpture of Philip II

Soldiers

Philip II made Macedonian soldiers the best in Greece. They fought with spears 5 metres long and had well-made body armour. The Macedonian army used large wooden catapults in battle to hurl rocks at their enemies.

Armour found in the tomb thought to belong to Philip II

Philip's tomb

A Macedonian tomb was found at Vergina in 1977. Inside was a golden chest containing the remains of a man. Scientists reconstructed his face, and it turned out to have a severe wound over the right eye. Philip had lost his right eye in battle, so archaeologists believe this is likely to have been his tomb.

Alexander the Great

Alexander was the son and heir of Philip of Macedonia. Alexander was a brilliant soldier who fulfilled his father's ambition to conquer an enormous empire. But Alexander's empire quickly fell apart after his early death.

War against Persia

Alexander led his Macedonian troops into Asia Minor (modern Turkey) in 334 BC. He had about 35,000 soldiers but the Persian king, Darius III, had many more. Despite this, Alexander's army defeated Darius at Issus in 333 BC – although Darius himself escaped.

In 332 BC Alexander and his army marched to Egypt and took control there. Returning to Persia, Alexander's troops met Darius's forces again at Gaugamela. There was another huge battle and the Persian army was destroyed. Alexander was crowned king of Persia in 331 BC.

GREECE

Alexander's Empire

PERSIA

Athens

Issus • Gaugamela
Babylon

• Persepolis

Alexandria

EGYPT

Top Facts

- Darius escaped after being defeated at the Battle of Gaugamela, but he was killed later by his own guards.

- The Macedonians founded many cities in the lands they conquered. Several were called Alexandria after Alexander.

Soldiers revolt

The Macedonians carried on, marching up into Central Asia, through Persia and down into India. Alexander's army travelled through the moutainous territory called the Hindu Kush. This was too far for the soldiers and they refused to go on. Alexander was forced to turn back.

The Hindu Kush

A mosaic showing Alexander the Great in battle

The Ishtar Gate in Babylon

The death of Alexander

While returning to Persia, Alexander developed a fever and died in Babylon in 323 BC. He was 32. After Alexander died, rival generals took control of parts of the Macedonian empire. Ptolemy governed Egypt, and his descendants ruled the country until the death of Cleopatra in AD 30. Antigonas ruled Macedonia and controlled Greece. Seleucus tried to govern the Middle East and Central Asia. Alexander's empire had collapsed.

Religion and temples

The Ancient Greeks worshipped gods they liked or whose help they needed. They believed the gods and goddesses would look after them in return for offerings.

Did You Know?

The Greek gods and goddesses behaved like people. They argued and fought, fell in love and got married. They often had direct contact with people and many of the heroes in Greek legends had a god as a parent.

Worship

Temples were built as places for the gods to live and each temple was linked with particular gods or goddesses. Most people worshipped at small altars in their homes rather than at the temple and only priests were allowed to enter the temple. People gathered outside the temple during festivals to make sacrifices in honour of the gods.

The temple of Neptune, below, is one of three large Greek temples at Paestum, a Greek colony founded in southern Italy in about 700 BC. The site is about 80 kilometres south of modern Naples.

The temple of Neptune at Paestum

Beautiful temples

Since temples were the houses of the gods, they were built of the best materials, including stone and marble. Temples were richly decorated with painted sculptures and even carved roof tiles. At the centre there was usually a statue of the god to which the temple was dedicated. In the back part of the temple was a room where precious offerings were stored.

Zeus and some of the more important gods were thought to live high on Mount Olympus, which no human was allowed to visit.

Top facts

- Sometimes temples were like a huge offering, built to thank a god or goddess for a victory in war.

- Different gods had to be prayed to in different ways, and needed sacrifices of different kinds of animals.

Columns

Most temples were surrounded by rows of columns which had carved tops called capitals.

Gods and goddesses

The Greeks had many gods and goddesses. Here are some of the most important, but there were many more.

A painting of Apollo in his chariot dating from the 1870s

Zeus

Zeus was the ruler of the gods. He was married to his sister Hera, but is said to have had many children with human women. He kept order in the world.

Athene

Athene was the goddess of wisdom and war, and was Zeus's daughter. She was also the goddess of the city of Athens.

Apollo

Apollo was a sun god, and was the god of truth, the arts and music. He was also responsible for healing.

Artemis

Artemis, huntress and goddess of the Moon, was Apollo's sister. She looked after girls and pregnant women.

Aphrodite

Aphrodite was the goddess of beauty and love. Her good looks caused a lot of jealousy and arguments – even wars.

Poseidon

Poseidon was the king of the oceans and controlled storms at sea. He was a very important god in a country with so many islands.

Hermes

Hermes was the gods' messenger. People worshipped him if they were setting out on a journey.

Demeter

Demeter was the goddess of the Earth. She also looked after growing things and harvests with her daughter Persephone.

Hera

Hera was the wife of Zeus. She protected women and marriage.

A wall painting of Aphrodite dating from the first century AD

Hades

Hades was the ruler of the underworld. People tried not to say his real name out loud and called him Pluto instead.

Dionysus

Dionysus was the son of Zeus and was the god of vines, wine and the theatre.

A carving showing Poseidon, Athene, Apollo and Artemis

Did You Know?

Each god or goddess was linked to certain things or symbols. An owl, for instance, often represented Athene, and the bird was shown on the coins of the city of Athens. The coins were even called 'owls'.

Oracles and festivals

Gods and goddesses were very close to the Ancient Greeks. The people believed that they could strike bargains with the gods.

Oracles

People talked to their gods. They thought the gods talked back, using a priest or priestess, called an oracle, as a mouthpiece. The most famous oracle was at Delphi, where the god Apollo spoke through a priestess called the Pythia.

The priestess forecast the future, and was so famous that many people asked her advice – even kings from faraway countries. She could only be visited during a very short period every year – originally just one day.

Aegeus, the king of Athens, consulting the Oracle at Delphi

Did You Know?

The Oracle at Delphi was not always clear about what she meant. One ruler, Croesus of Lydia, is supposed to have asked her what would happen if he fought Persia. She told him that he would destroy a great empire, so he went ahead – and he lost. The empire he destroyed was his own.

Top Facts

- Anyone wishing to visit the oracle at Delphi had to make valuable offerings – and pay a large fee as well.

- Another way of seeing the future was to read omens, or signs. These could be things such as the way a flock of birds flew or the pattern made by lightning.

The remains of the temple at Delphi

Festivals

Festivals were a way of bargaining with the gods, or thanking them. They could be held to persuade the gods to protect a city, ensure a good harvest or grant the wishes of a wealthy person.

Some festivals were small, but others were enormous. They included music, singing, dancing, plays, processions, plenty of food and drink and religious ceremonies – when people offered animals as sacrifices to the gods. Most happened at the same time of year, every year or every four years.

The games at Olympia

Athletic contests were another way of honouring the gods, and were often part of a religious festival. The most famous games were at Olympia.

Zeus's festival

Every four years there was a famous competition at Olympia – a holy place connected to the god Zeus. It lasted for five days and the best athletes travelled there from all over Greece. Later the competition was opened to foreigners too. On the last day of the games simple wreaths of laurel leaves were given as prizes.

Athletic events

The games began with running contests, but there were many other events. Wrestling, a very violent form of boxing called *pankration*, jumping, and throwing the discus and javelin were all popular.

A carving of wrestlers

Racing with horses

There were also horse and chariot races. Chariot racing was probably the most exciting. Two or four horses pulled each chariot, and up to 40 chariots could compete at once. There were lots of dramatic crashes.

Top Facts

- The games at Olympia were so important by the seventh century BC that wars were stopped so that people could travel to Olympia.

- Women competed in a separate games called the Heraea – but there was only one race for them to take part in.

The Palaistra

The Palaistra, or exercise ground, was where boxers and wrestlers trained. It consisted of an open courtyard surrounded by a shaded area called the colonnade and rooms for teaching and storage. The remains of the pillars of the colonnade can be seen here.

Running

Races were run on a track, which was about 192 metres long. Sprinters ran one length of the track and long-distance runners could run up to 24 lengths.

Did You Know?

Almost anything went in the fighting event called pankration, except biting or gouging your opponent's eyes out. Fights could last for hours and result in serious injuries because the fighters wore leather straps studded with metal. Some contestants even died.

Working life

Most Ancient Greeks were farmers, but men could also become craftsmen, merchants, sailors or builders. Jobs that were heavy, dirty or even dangerous were done by slaves.

Top Facts

- Officials checked up on traders, making sure they were giving the right quantities and not cheating their customers.
- Olive oil was used for many things other than cooking, such as medicine, cosmetics, washing and lighting.

Craftsmen

Skilled craftsmen made beautiful things such as pots and metalwork. Pots were painted with scenes from myths and everyday life. Much of what we know about life in Ancient Greece comes from the pictures on these pots.

Weapons were made of metal and so were sculptures and jewellery. Most metalworkers had small workshops near their homes.

Some Greeks were also skilled carpenters and leather workers, but their work has not survived.

A group of workers harvesting olives is shown on this large pot.

Farming and trading

Although there were farms in the countryside around Athens, these farms were small and most food for the city had to come from further away – even from abroad. Merchant ships brought everything, from grain to metal ore, into the port of Piraeus.

Goods were sold in the market-place, either from temporary stalls or from shops. There would be food, such as fruit, vegetables, oil, fish and meat (displayed on marble slabs to keep them cool), and wine. Slaves were also bought at the market.

Did You Know?

Slaves helped out at the training grounds where men went to exercise. Men always practised and competed without clothes. After they finished slaves rubbed them down with olive oil.

Slaves

Household slaves did jobs such as cleaning, cooking – like the woman in this sculpture – and fetching water. They also looked after their owners, helping them to get dressed and serving food. A special slave took boys to school and watched them doing lessons.

Slaves also worked in silver mines and workshops and often had a hard life. They could be tortured if they were suspected of a crime. It was thought they could not be trusted to tell the truth.

Family life

Men were always at the head of the family, and they made the rules. Women hardly went out of their homes, and children, especially boys, were very important.

Sculpture of a girl

Boys

Boys would grow up to become citizens. Schooling was quite expensive so only the sons of rich people could be educated. Most boys needed to help their fathers from an early age, and they were thought to be young adults from about the age of 12. Keeping fit was very important because boys had to grow up to be good soldiers, as well as doing things such as helping on the family farm, like the boy below.

Girls

Girls didn't go to school and were not usually taught to read and write. They could never own property or inherit money and had to leave their families when they got married. Girls normally married when they were 13 or 14. Their husbands were usually more than twice their age.

Women

Women were almost always controlled by men, either their fathers, brothers, husbands or sons, who told them what they could do. They mainly stayed at home, though they were allowed to visit their female friends.

Women ran the home, managing the money, organizing the slaves, spinning wool and weaving cloth. They looked after anyone who was ill, too. Poorer women got out more, to buy food or fetch water – and some even ran bars!

Some women lived independently as companions to wealthy men, but they were not thought to be respectable and had often started out as slaves.

This painting on a pot shows a woman entertaining a friend.

Getting dressed

The Ancient Greeks wore simple, comfortable clothing, although wealthy women often had beautiful jewellery.

Wrapping up

Both men and women wore clothes based on rectangles of cloth, often made from wool and sometimes linen. The sides were stitched together, leaving space at the top for the arms, and they were fastened over the shoulders with brooches or pins. A belt went round the waist and the cloth was pulled up over it. Men's tunics were knee length, while women's dresses touched the floor. People sometimes also wore cloaks. Women were supposed to keep their body covered and to cover their head if they went out.

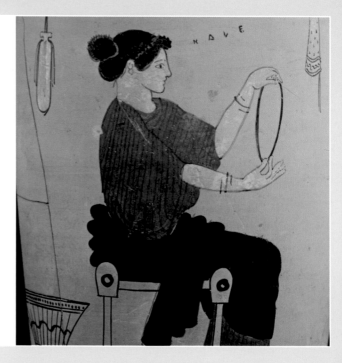

Hair

Women, except for slaves, usually had long hair. It was tied up in complicated styles with ribbons or scarves. Men often had beards, especially if they were older.

Did You Know?

Cloth was often dyed in bright colours. Many dyes came from plants, but not all. Purple was made from sea snails and it took nearly 10,000 snails to make one gram of dye. Dyed cloth was often treated with urine so the colour wouldn't run.

We can tell that this is a rich woman because she has a complicated hairstyle and lots of jewellery. She is looking in a mirror.

Top Facts

- Women stayed out of the sun. They thought suntans were ugly and used chalk to make their skin look pale.

- Most Greeks went barefoot or wore leather sandals with lots of straps.

Jewellery

Women had pierced ears, and archaeologists have found many earrings made from silver or gold. Rich women owned gold necklaces and bracelets as well, or wore gold in their hair. Most people would have had some pins or brooches for holding their clothes in place.

Earring

Eating and feasting

Food in Ancient Greece was often similar to what we eat today, but feasts could be very elaborate.

A cup dating from about 400 BC

Food

Most people filled up with porridge and bread, which was often made with barley rather than wheat. Fruit, vegetables, lentils and olives were also popular, as were fish and cheese. Meat was mainly eaten on special occasions such as religious festivals.

A plate dating from about 490 BC

Cups and plates

This cup is decorated with a picture of an owl – the symbol of the goddess Athene. Plates were often decorated with scenes from Greek mythology.

Did You Know?

Greek farmers kept sheep and goats for meat, milk and their skins. These animals could adapt well to living in the mountainous landscape.

Wine

Wine was everyone's favourite drink. It was usually mixed with water. At parties this would be done in a large pot called a *krater*, and a slave would then serve it out into cups or jugs using a ladle.

Feasting

Dinner was usually eaten late and was a chance to entertain. Men held banquets or drinking parties and women, except for slaves, were not allowed to be present. Guests often ate reclining on couches.

After the meal

The evening really began once the food was cleared away. Men began to discuss things like politics. Sometimes there were singers, storytellers or acrobats.

Did You Know?

Even serious dinner-party talk would get less sensible as guests drank more and more. Some cups had pointed bottoms so they couldn't be put down and had to be passed round until they were empty. Eventually the men would pass out and sleep on their couches while the slaves cleared up.

A scene showing people at a feast with a servant bringing a tray of fruit

Top Facts

- The Ancient Greeks sweetened their food with honey as there was no sugar.

- The Greeks didn't use forks. People scooped up their food using their fingers or pieces of bread.

Going to a play

Some theatres, and even plays, survive from Ancient Greece. Large numbers of people went to see plays – but historians think that women were not allowed to go to the theatre.

How plays began

Songs and dances were originally a part of religious festivals. After a while these became stories, and then the stories became more important. Soon they were turned into plays with several actors. A larger group of actors, called the Chorus, spoke directly to the audience.

Comedies and tragedies

There were two kinds of plays. Tragedies were serious stories about gods or heroes. Comedies had a lot of clowning and rude jokes, and often poked fun at politicians. The masks of comedy and tragedy (above) are still used today as a symbol for the theatre.

Top Facts

- All the actors were men, even those playing women.

- Ancient Greek plays such *Medea* by Euripides and *Antigone* by Sophocles are still performed today, sometimes using copies of the costumes and masks Ancient Greek actors would have used.

Theatres

Greek theatres were in the open. One of the most famous is at Epidauros. A big semicircle with slanting sides was dug into the hill. At the bottom was a flat area – the stage where the actors and the Chorus performed.

The sides of the semi-circle were lined with seats, and Epidauros could hold 14,000 people. It is so well designed that actors speaking on the stage can be heard clearly at the back, in the top row of seats.

Did You Know?

Because theatres were so large, people at the back couldn't see the actors' faces. So actors wore masks to show who they were playing and what sort of mood they were in. Dark costumes were used in tragedies and colourful clothes were used for people who were happy.

ANCIENT ROME

In the first century AD the Roman Empire stretched across Europe, from Spain to the Middle East, north to the borders of Scotland and south into Africa. We have learned a lot about life during the time of the Roman Empire from the remains of the cities of Pompeii and Herculaneum, which were buried by the eruption of Vesuvius in AD 79, and also from the ruins of villas, forts, baths and other Roman buildings that are spread across Europe and North Africa.

The beginning of Rome

About 3000 years ago, in the country we now call Italy, a few small villages built on hills above the River Tiber began to grow and join together. They eventually developed into a large walled city, full of important buildings. The city was called Rome and it eventually became the capital of the Roman Empire.

Ruling Rome

Early Rome was ruled by kings who were chosen by an assembly of respected older men called senators. Some of these kings were Etruscans – Rome's powerful neighbours. The Etruscan kings were unpopular, and the last king, Tarquin, was particularly disliked because he wanted to rule without the advice of the senators. Tarquin was driven out by the people of Rome in 510 BC. After this, Rome was governed by the senators and became a republic – that is, a state governed by elected rulers.

Hannibal

Over time Rome grew more powerful, but it was threatened by Carthage, a powerful state in North Africa. In 219 BC Hannibal, a general from Carthage, crossed into Spain with his armies. The following year Hannibal's army, accompanied by 37 war elephants, marched through France and into Italy across the Alps. Hannibal won many battles but was eventually defeated after the Romans attacked his home city of Carthage.

In 146 BC the Romans burned the city of Carthage and Rome became the strongest power in the Mediterranean. Roman generals became very powerful, too. They brought riches to back to Rome, but they also brought their soldiers and fought each other for power.

A Roman myth

Some Romans believed their city had been founded by Romulus and Remus, twins who had been abandoned as babies and brought up by a wolf. This statue shows Romulus and Remus being nursed by a she-wolf.

The first emperor

As Rome became more powerful, generals fought each other for control. Ordinary people suffered as their houses and crops were destroyed, and many were killed in the battles until Augustus brought peace to Rome.

Julius Caesar

One of the most powerful of the Roman generals was Julius Caesar (c. 100–44 BC), who had conquered Gaul (now called France). Julius Caesar gradually defeated the other generals, taking more and more power, until he eventually ruled Rome and its growing empire.

As he took more power, some senators thought Julius Caesar was behaving too much like one of the hated kings. A group of them killed him in 44 BC.

Top Facts

- At first the position of emperor was passed on through families. This changed when the Emperor Nerva adopted Trajan as his son so that Trajan could rule after his death in AD 98.

- Being emperor could be a dangerous job. The three emperors following Augustus were all murdered.

This picture, painted in 1899, shows Vercingetorix, leader of the Gauls, surrendering to Julius Caesar in 52 BC.

Augustus

More wars broke out after Julius Caesar's death but Octavian, Caesar's adopted son, eventually won control. In 27 BC, Octavian changed his name to Augustus. Augustus, supported by the army, ruled the Roman Empire for 41 years. Historians usually call him 'the first Roman Emperor', although he did not use the title 'emperor' himself. After Augustus, emperors governed Rome for the next 400 years. Many did not rule as wisely as Augustus had.

Did You Know?

After Augustus died, his stepson Tiberius became emperor. He left Rome for the island of Capri, thinking people wanted to kill him — unwelcome visitors were thrown off the cliffs of Capri.

Nero

Emperor Nero (ruling AD 54–68) had many people killed, including his mother and wife. He believed he was a great musician and gave long concerts that people had to attend. They were not allowed to leave before the end — some would even pretend to die so they could be carried out. A terrible fire destroyed much of Rome in AD 64, and people thought Nero had started it so he could build a new city on the ruins.

The Roman Empire

The Roman Empire eventually stretched for thousands of kilometres, becoming one of the greatest the world had ever seen.

Other lands

Victory over Carthage in 146 BC brought large parts of North Africa under Roman control, and there were many other victories further east. Julius Caesar conquered Gaul (France) and Augustus added Egypt.

Caesar invaded Britannia (now called Britain) in 55 BC, but it was only a raid and he retreated. In AD 43, during the reign of the Emperor Claudius, the Roman armies returned and conquered the British tribes.

Roman style

People all over the empire copied Roman fashions and ways of living. This Roman-style mosaic is in a synagogue in Tunisia.

Trajan's Column

Trajan's Column in Rome was built in AD 113 to honour the victories of the Emperor Trajan.

Emperor Trajan

The Emperor Trajan (AD 98–117) was a great general and led the Roman army on many campaigns, often at the very edge of the empire. He gained control of Dacia (modern Romania) and huge areas in the east – Armenia, Assyria and Mesopotamia.

A vast Empire

By the first century AD, Rome ruled a vast area, and more than 50 million people lived under its rule. Such a huge empire was difficult to control and there were often wars as local people rebelled against their Roman overlords.

The Roman amphitheatre at El Djem in Tunisia, North Africa

BRITANNIA

Atlantic Ocean

GAUL

DACIA

HISPANIA

Rome

ARMENIA

MESOPOTAMIA

ASSYRIA

Mediterranean Sea

Africa

EGYPT

Trajan's empire

Trajan's empire stretched from southern Scotland to the deserts of North Africa, and from the Atlantic Coast of Spain and Portugal right across to Asia.

Hadrian's Walls

The Emperor Hadrian built fortifications in many places to defend the Roman Empire against the hostile tribes who lived beyond its frontiers.

Hadrian's Wall

Newcastle upon Tyne

Carlisle

BRITANNIA

The Emperor

When Hadrian became emperor after the death of Trajan in AD 117, he decided that some of Trajan's conquests were just too far away to be ruled easily. He abandoned them and began building fortifications on the new borders.

He added a wooden wall and more forts to the frontiers in Germany. Then he did something new in Britannia (Britain). He marked the northern boundary of the Roman Empire with a tall stone wall, over 5 metres high.

Hadrian's Wall

This wall, now named after the emperor, ran right across northern Britain from coast to coast, stretching for about 113 kilometres. In the middle of the country it was built on top of high cliffs, making it seem even taller.

Top Facts

- Many of the troops who patrolled Hadrian's Wall were not Roman. There were some from Germany, and men even came from Syria.

- When it was first built Hadrian's Wall was painted white, probably to make it look even more impressive.

Roman toilets

Roman toilets can still be seen at Housesteads fort. The seats were built above the drains, which you can see around the edges of the room. The Romans used sponges on sticks instead of toilet paper.

Modern copy of a watch tower

Original Roman remains

The wall forts

A huge flat-bottomed ditch lay just behind the wall, and forts of different sizes were built all the way along – like this one at Housesteads. Other forts lay a short distance behind the wall, and good roads linked everything to the military centre further south at York.

Vindolanda fort

There is a modern copy of a watch tower at Vindolanda fort, so we can see what the original would have looked like.

The city of Rome

Rome was the capital city of a huge empire. Nearly a million people lived in Rome by the first century BC.

Great buildings

The Forum was the centre of Rome. It was an open space used for meetings and markets and was surrounded by important buildings. There were temples, law courts and a building called the *Curia*, where the senate gathered. Nearby were the Colosseum and theatres, where the Roman people went to be entertained. The Emperor Augustus, like most later emperors, built magnificent monuments, such as temples, arches and theatres, so that he would be remembered.

Top Facts

- Many rich Romans liked to leave the city for the summer, because the risk of disease was highest at that time. They moved to their country houses.

- Rome was very dangerous at night. There were no street lights, and mugging and burglaries were common. And so was murder.

This arch, near the Colosseum, was built by the Emperor Constantine in AD 315.

Living in the city

The houses of the rich were luxurious, but most people lived in very different conditions. Many had their homes in badly built apartment buildings. Only wealthy houses were connected to the drains and so disease spread easily in the poor parts of the city. There were no organized rubbish collections – so the city must have smelled bad, especially in summer.

Trajan's Rome

This marketplace was built by Emperor Trajan, who ruled AD 98–117. The marketplace was surrounded by shops and offices.

The Fire of Rome

Roman houses were often built using wood. They were heated with small oil stoves and lit by oil lamps, so fire was a big danger. Emperor Augustus organized teams of watchmen (called *vigiles*) to act as firefighters. With only buckets and small hand pumps they were not very good at putting out the fires. A huge fire destroyed two thirds of the city in AD 64.

A Roman oil lamp

125

Vesuvius erupts

On 24 August AD 79 the volcano Mount Vesuvius erupted, burying the nearby Roman cities of Pompeii and Herculaneum under a blanket of hot ash.

A cloud of ash

The busy cities of Pompeii and Herculaneum lay south of Rome, on the Bay of Naples. There had been a serious earthquake in the area a few years before the eruption, and there were small ones just before 24 August, but life went on as normal. Then Vesuvius erupted.

At about midday the whole top of the mountain was blown away. Huge clouds of ash and rock were thrown miles up into the sky in a series of massive explosions lasting about 20 hours. Some people managed to get away – but soon ash clouds were raining down on the two cities and there was little chance of escape.

Top Facts

- Over a thousand years after the eruption, people began digging in the area. They made some amazing discoveries about life in Roman times.

- When the ash clouds settled, the whole landscape had changed. Not only had the towns vanished, but the line of the coast itself had altered.

The town of Pompeii today, with Mount Vesuvius behind it

Forgotten cities

When the eruption ended, Pompeii was buried beneath about 5 metres of ash, with only the tips of the tallest roofs showing. Those who had escaped found new homes, many in nearby Naples and, over time, people forgot that the towns had ever existed.

The figures

When people died, their bodies were buried in the hardening ash and rock. Over time the bodies decayed, leaving a hollow. Years later, the hollows were carefully filled with plaster, making perfect plaster casts of the people who once lay there. There are casts of animals, too.

Life in Pompeii and Herculaneum

These forgotten towns were rediscovered in the 1700s. The blanket of ash and volcanic dust helped preserve them so that we can see what life might have been like in Roman times.

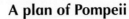

A plan of Pompeii

Vesuvius Gate
Capua Gate
Herculaneum Gate
Nola Gate
Sarno Gate
Marina Gate
Nucerian Gate
Stabian Gate

Buildings
Unexcavated Areas

Houses and gardens

Some of the houses in Pompeii and Herculaneum were very large and beautifully decorated with wall paintings and mosaics. Many had gardens, where the Romans grew herbs, vines, fruit trees and vegetables as well as decorative plants such as oleander and myrtle.

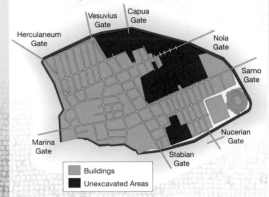

A mosaic from Pompeii shows entertainers working in the street.

Shops

There were shops selling food and drink, and plenty of bars. Here we can see a baker's oven and a millstone in Pompeii. Flour was made by grinding wheat between the heavy millstones, which were turned by donkeys. Archaeologists have found a house that belonged to a doctor. They know this because there were many medicial instruments inside.

Top Facts

- Pompeii probably had a population of about 20,000 people at the time of the eruption. The town of Herculaneum was much smaller, with a population of about 4000 people.

- Vesuvius is still an active volcano. It last erupted in 1944, though not as badly as in Roman times.

Did You Know?

We even know what the people of Pompeii ate as, in some places, food was found on tables. There were round loaves of bread looking just like the bread we eat today. Pomegranates, grape pips, cherry stones and fig seeds were also discovered.

Decoration

The House of the Mysteries is richly decorated with bright wall paintings. It shows us what the house of a rich person would have looked like.

Building and engineering

The Romans left their mark all over the empire, designing and building roads, bridges, forts, baths and even drains wherever they settled.

Technology

Roman builders used stone and fired bricks. They also invented concrete – a strong volcanic dust called *pozzolana* was mixed with water and rubble. The resulting concrete was strong, easy to use, quite light and lasted well. It was used to fill the middle of walls, so tall structures could be built with no risk of collapse.

A Roman dome

Roman architects and builders invented the dome. This magnificent dome is part of the Pantheon – a Roman temple that still stands in Rome. Today it is a Christian church, which attracts visitors from around the world.

Did You Know?
Roman cities had good water supplies. There were public fountains fed by aqueducts and water channels.

The massive Pont du Gard aqueduct in Gaul, now called France, carried water to the city of Nimes.

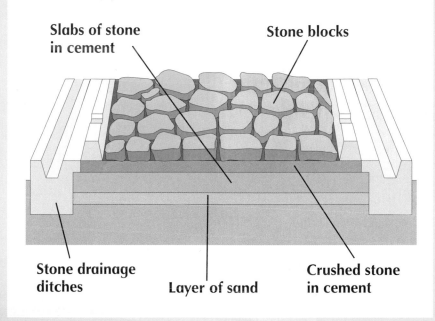

Roman roads were built in layers.

Slabs of stone in cement

Stone blocks

Stone drainage ditches

Layer of sand

Crushed stone in cement

The Romans built round arches in buildings, bridges and aqueducts.

Floor

Channels carrying hot air

Heating

Some public buildings and larger houses, such as this villa at Chedworth in the south of England, had underfloor heating. This was particularly important in bathhouses. A furnace in the basement, stoked by slaves, sent hot air through gaps under the floors. Floors could sometimes get very hot – too hot for bare feet – so bathers had to wear wooden sandals.

The Roman army

Without the huge Roman army, the Empire would never have been conquered or controlled. It was the world's first real full-time army, and it was feared by Rome's enemies.

First full-time soldiers

In the early days, the Roman army was made up of conscripts – men who were called up to fight at times of war. But as Rome grew in power and influence, professional soldiers were needed full time to protect its borders against invaders. These soldiers were specially trained and spent most of their lives in the army.

Marius's mules

Until 107 BC, you had to own land to be in the Roman army. But General Marius wanted to expand the army so he allowed poorer men to join. Soldiers began to get proper pay and were well trained. They had good weapons and equipment but they had to carry these everywhere. Because of this they called themselves 'Marius's mules'.

Top Facts

- The army was so powerful that emperors made sure they kept their soldiers happy so that they remained loyal.

- By the second century AD there were about 150,000 soldiers in the Roman army.

Emperor Trajan was a great commander.

This sculpture shows a soldier with his main weapon – a short sword.

Roman legions

The army was made up of legions. Each legion had about 5000–6000 foot soldiers. These were divided into units of 480 men called cohorts. Each cohort was made up of six 'centuries' of 80 men led by a centurion.

Specialist soldiers

There were many non-Roman troops, too, called auxiliaries. They were often foreigners, such as the horseback archers from Palmyra in Syria, who had skills that the Romans lacked. They often served a long way from their homes and were made citizens of Rome when they retired after 26 years' service.

These men are dressed as Roman soldiers.

A soldier's life

Life in the army was hard, so Roman soldiers had to be tough. They were away from home for years at a time and they risked being killed in war. But there was more to military life than fighting battles.

Arms and armour

All soldiers wore some body armour and a helmet, and officers' helmets had special crests. Armour was usually made from overlapping strips of iron attached to leather straps. A soldier carried a heavy javelin, a short sword, a dagger and a big square shield. In battle, groups of men would sometimes form into a square and lock their shields together along the sides and over their heads. This formation was called a 'tortoise' and protected them from missiles such as arrows and spears.

Old Sarum Roman fortress in England

Marching

The legions could march very fast. They surprised their enemies by arriving before they were expected, which gave them a real advantage. They kept up a steady pace, marching up to 30 kilometres a day when the roads were well built like the one shown on the left. They built temporary bridges so they could cross rivers, and every night they set up a fortified camp.

Did You Know?

As well as weapons, the men also carried their kit. This included a pack containing personal items, a pan, dish, toolkit, water bottle, cloak and digging tools. Good footwear was vital, and Roman soldiers had shoes with nailed soles and lots of straps over the top of the feet for ventilation.

Life in a Roman fort

Many soldiers acted as frontier guards, based in permanent forts. The soldiers weren't allowed to marry, but many had unofficial wives and children. Family settlements often grew up just outside forts.

A trumpet call started every day, calling soldiers to duty. Training was hard. The men practised throwing javelins and fighting, but also had to exercise to keep themselves fit. There were other jobs, too. Many soldiers were trained as engineers and builders.

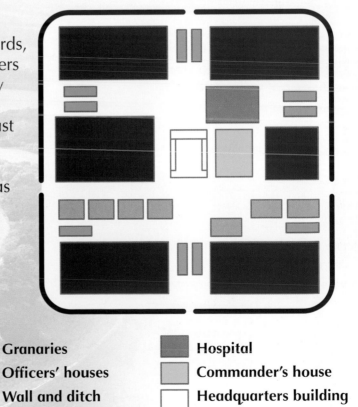

- ■ **Barrack blocks**
- ■ **Barracks with houses for centurions**
- ■ **Granaries**
- ■ **Officers' houses**
- ▬ **Wall and ditch**
- ■ **Hospital**
- ■ **Commander's house**
- □ **Headquarters building**

Travel and trade

As the empire grew, it became ever more important to be able to travel quickly, so that soldiers could reach distant provinces, the emperor could send messages to his troops and merchants were able to trade.

Moving about the empire

Many roads had been built by soldiers so they could reach their destinations quickly. But other people used them, too, on foot, riding horses or using donkeys, mules and carts to carry their goods. There were big wooden carts for heavy loads and lighter, faster two-wheeled chariots to carry people.

Trade

Without trade Rome could not have flourished, or even have fed its people. Everything was traded, from precious materials such as amber, metal and wood to food and drink, such as oil, fish, grain and wine, and fabric. Silk even came from China, traded along the Silk Road.

A Roman road in central Spain

Top Facts

- The same money was used almost everywhere in the empire, which made buying and selling easy.

- Several wrecks of Roman ships have been found, so we know what goods they carried. One ship was bringing heavy stone coffins to Italy.

The port of Ostia

Goods were often moved by ship, even though sea voyages could be dangerous. Boats were also used on inland rivers. They were especially important for moving cargo on the River Tiber – the river that linked Rome to the sea at Ostia.

A large artificial harbour was built at Ostia so boats could be unloaded safely. Huge quantities of food and drink came into the port. About 1000 boatloads of grain were needed to feed the people of Rome every year. They had to be transported from the sea at Ostia, up the River Tiber all the way to Rome.

Did You Know?

Some of the most dangerous cargoes must have been the wild animals used in the Games, which were sent from Africa and Asia. There were lions, leopards, elephants, rhinoceroses and smaller animals such as antelopes.

Giant warehouses

In Ostia much of the cargo was stored in gigantic warehouses. One warehouse had as many as 140 rooms! Warehouses had thick walls and tiny windows to make it difficult for thieves to break in.

Sunken cargo

This diver is holding a Roman container called an *amphora*, which might have contained oil or wine. It was found at the bottom of the Mediterranean Sea.

137

Religion and temples

The Romans worshipped many different gods, and throughout the Roman Empire there were many other local gods, who were also important.

The temple to Jupiter, king of the gods, in Tunisia, North Africa

Gods of Rome

Everyone in the empire was expected to respect and honour the gods of Rome. As long as they did that, they could also worship their own local gods and goddesses. Jews and Christians, who believed in one god, refused to honour the Roman gods and so they were punished.

Temples

This temple in Nimes, France, is one of the best-preserved of all Roman temples. Temples were seen as the houses of the gods and most ceremonies happened outside them, where people could see them and join in. Sometimes statues of gods or goddesses, which were usually kept inside the temple, would be paraded around the street in grand processions.

Did You Know?

There were many Roman festivals but Saturnalia was special. It took place between 17 and 23 December. There were lots of parties with eating and drinking.

Top Facts

- The emperor was the chief priest of Rome. He was given the title Pontifex Maximus.

- There were many superstitions, and days that were thought to be either lucky or unlucky. Charms were used to protect people from evil and most people believed in the power of curses.

Emperors

Augustus was declared to be a god shortly after he died. Many other rulers later became gods, and temples were built to them after their deaths. Worshipping a dead emperor was a way of respecting Rome and being patriotic.

Everyday gods and offerings

Roman houses had shrines to Lares and Penates, the household gods who protected the home. The Romans prayed and made small offerings, such as food or wine, to these gods. More important gods needed bigger offerings if they were to protect people or bring good luck, and animal sacrifices were common.

A household shrine from Pompeii

Gods and goddesses

Many of the most important Roman gods were similar to the Ancient Greek gods. The Romans used the stories created by the Greeks but gave their gods Roman names. Romans worshipped gods from other places, too – the Egyptian goddess Isis was popular, for example. Here are some of the most important ones.

A mosaic showing Minerva, dating from 1880

Jupiter

Jupiter was, like the Greek god Zeus, ruler of the gods. He controlled the sky and gave warnings – and punishments – to humans.

Juno

Juno was the equivalent of the Greek goddess Hera. She was Jupiter's wife and protected women.

Minerva

Minerva was worshipped by soldiers as well as many others. She would have been called Athena by the Ancient Greeks.

Mars

Mars, god of war, was very important in Rome. Generals made offerings to him before they left to fight, and again when they returned.

Saturn

Saturn was the god of farming. His festival, the Saturnalia, was a chance for everyone to enjoy themselves and have a huge party.

Vesta

Vesta, goddess of the hearth, was served by six noble priestesses called the Vestal Virgins. They had to serve her for 30 years and were not allowed to marry. If they broke their vows they put Rome in danger and could be buried alive as a punishment.

Did You Know?

Some months or days of the week get their names from Roman gods or goddesses. Saturn gave his name to Saturday; June comes from Juno and March from Mars. January, the first month of the year, comes from Janus – the god of new beginnings. August is named after Augustus and July after Julius Caesar.

Cybele

Cybele, the Great Mother, was originally an eastern goddess. Ceremonies in her temples involved gory rituals and she had special priests to perform these. Many people were shocked by them.

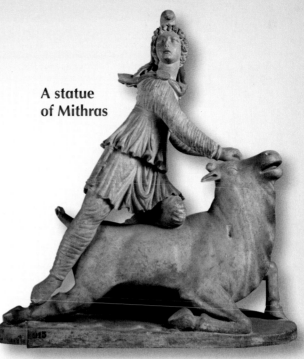

A statue of Mithras

Mithras

Mithras was worshipped by men, mostly soldiers or ex-soldiers, in mysterious ceremonies. They were so secret that nobody knows exactly what they were. Mithras was a Persian god, but his cult spread all over the empire.

Venus

Venus was the goddess of love and beauty, like the Greek goddess Aphrodite. She was very popular and had many shrines where people could leave offerings.

Isis

Isis was an Egyptian goddess who was worshipped throughout the Roman world, especially in places where traders gathered.

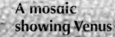

A mosaic showing Venus

People of the Roman Empire

There were rich people and poor people in Roman society, but it was possible to improve your position. Slaves could become free men (called freedmen), and many important citizens had slave ancestors.

Citizens

People were divided into Roman citizens and non-citizens. Citizens had more rights but were also expected to serve the state in some way. In early times citizens were only those who had actually been born in Rome, but later more people qualified. You could gain citizenship by serving the state.

These portraits from Pompeii show a young man and woman. She is holding a writing tablet, so we know that they were rich.

Top Facts

- Nearly a third of the people in Italy were slaves in the first century AD, and about half the people in Rome were either slaves or freedmen.

- Many slaves were Celts from Britain or Gaul (now France). One chief from Gaul is said to have traded people for wine.

Slaves

Slaves, like this noblewoman's servant, had no rights at all and could be bought and sold. They ran homes, farmed the land and worked in their masters' businesses. Some, often educated Greeks, were secretaries and advisers and could even work closely with the emperor. Sometimes slaves became freedmen – a master might free his slaves after his death and some slaves were able to save enough money to buy their freedom.

Patricians and plebians

Citizens were either nobles, called patricians, or plebians, who made up the majority of the population. Many plebians (often called plebs) were poor, but others worked as craftsmen or ran shops like this baker (right). Some plebians, called equites (meaning knights), became rich merchants or bankers because they were allowed to trade, unlike patricians. The plebs eventually gained some power from the patricians, and some became senators.

Family life

Fathers controlled their families, but mothers ran the home. Many would have had help from servants or slaves.

Fathers

Men had power over their wives, children and slaves, but there's evidence to show that fathers seem to have been remembered fondly by their children. A father's property was divided equally between all his children when he died.

Mothers

Women were expected to be good, quiet wives and mothers. They weren't allowed to play any part in public life (although many richer ones did, behind the scenes) and were only supposed to run the house. Widows, especially if they were wealthy, had more independence. Poorer women worked, often running shops, and many were slaves.

A wall painting at Pompeii shows a mother and her son.

Top Facts

- Children often died young. Diseases that are easy to cure now were deadly then. Living conditions were often difficult, especially for the poor.

- Many houses had guard dogs, and some dogs wore identity tags in case they got lost.

A copy of a Roman toy horse with wheels

Toys

Lots of Roman toys have been found. Children played with wooden swords, dolls, model cars and chariots. They also enjoyed a game of marbles!

Did You Know?

In early times, fathers could punish their children by selling them as slaves. Laws were eventually passed to stop this happening.

School

Schools were for boys from rich families. Lessons in reading, writing and maths started early, at dawn, and finished about noon. Pupils were frequently beaten and the lessons had to be learned by heart. Girls usually only had a basic education; they were expected to learn how to keep a house. Poorer children went straight to work as soon as they were able to do so.

A sculpture showing a school scene

Roman homes

Wealthy people often had homes both in the city and in the countryside. Some Roman houses were enormous, just like palaces. Poorer people lived more simply, many in apartment blocks.

Fine houses

Noble families had luxurious homes. These houses had a central courtyard called an atrium, which was open to the sky. It had a pool in the floor which caught rainwater. Rooms opened off the atrium. Large houses often had garden courtyards, too. Walls were painted in bright colours and floors were covered in mosaic designs. Country houses, called villas, could be even more lavish than town houses.

A Roman house

Most large Roman houses followed a similar plan. Small shops often occupied the rooms at the front of the house.

- Entrance hall
- Shops
- Pool
- Atrium
- Small rooms
- Dining room
- Kitchen
- Shaded garden
- Garden
- Study

Apartments

Roman apartment blocks, called *insulae*, could be up to seven storeys tall. Lower-floor apartments were often spacious and comfortable, but flats got smaller the higher up they were. The poorest people lived at the top.

Hadrian's Villa

The emperor Hadrian built a gigantic villa outside Rome at Tivoli, which covered an area twice as big as the town of Pompeii. There were many large buildings and beautiful gardens (right), as well as storerooms, warehouses and offices. A network of underground passages linked parts of the villa.

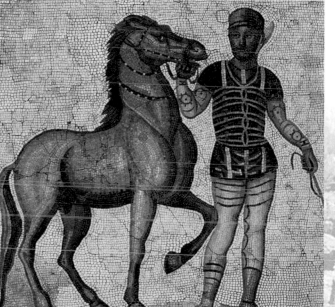

Mosaics

Mosaic floors were made up of lots of differently coloured small cubes of stone or pottery. A design was drawn and individual cubes, called *tesserae*, were pressed into wet cement to make up the pattern or picture. They were hard-wearing, and many still survive in almost perfect condition.

A mosaic of a chariot racer and his horse

The remains of *insulae* in the port of Ostia

147

Reading and writing

Many languages were spoken in the Roman Empire, but Latin, the language of Rome, was used throughout the empire.

Speaking to us

We can see still see many examples of Roman writing today. Inscriptions on monuments tell us when and why they were put up, and there are also fragments of ordinary letters or accounts.

Records were vital to the running of the empire. Some have survived at places such as Vindolanda fort on Hadrian's Wall. At Vindolanda archaeologists have found thousands of records written on thin pieces of wood. These tell us about how the forts were organized. There are also personal letters, which even include an invitation to a birthday party.

Stylus   Wax tablet

Letters and notes

There was no paper in Rome and Egyptian papyrus was expensive, so wax tablets were often used for writing. Warm wax was poured into a wooden frame and allowed to set, it could then be written on using a metal point called a stylus. The woman in this painting is holding a wax tablet and stylus. Once the message was read the wax could be softened and reused. Sometimes, thin pieces of wood or animal skins were written on with ink made from soot and water.

The Roman calendar

In 46–45 BC Julius Caesar ruled that every year would have 365 days, and that there would be an extra day every fourth year. We still follow this rule today – the year with the extra day, 29 February, is called a leap year. We also divide the year into 12 months like the Romans did.

Books

Generally books were long scrolls made of animal skins, which had to be unwound and rewound, but the very first books with pages were made in Roman times. Scrolls were rare and valuable, and most people would never have seen one. Stories and poems were read aloud at home and in public places such as the baths.

Dressing up

All Romans liked to look good if they could! Both men and women spent money – and time – on clothes, hair and make-up.

Men

All men, including slaves, usually wore simple tunics made from two pieces of cloth stitched together and belted at the waist. Richer citizens might wear a cloak over their tunic. Togas could only be worn by citizens. They were semi-circular pieces of cloth nearly 3 metres long which were wound about a man's body and draped over one shoulder. They were awkward and uncomfortable so most citizens only wore them occasionally. Underneath some men wore a loincloth – a strip of fabric – as underwear.

This mosaic shows men draped in togas.

A wall painting of a citizen wearing a toga

Jewellery

Many Romans wore jewellery, from simple rings for men to women's ankle chains. Rich women would own many necklaces, earrings and bracelets.

A Roman earring made of gold

Hair

Hairstyles could be very complicated. They were created by skilled slaves. Baldness was sometimes hidden by a wig.

Women

Like men, women sometimes wore a loincloth as underwear. Some of them also wore a fabric or leather bra. Long, loose tunic dresses were worn over the underwear, held in at the waist by a belt. Dresses were often in bright colours and could be made of fine material, even rare Chinese silk. On top of the dress went a large shawl, which was wound round the body and draped over one shoulder.

Eating and drinking

Most people ate simple, ordinary foods that we would recognize today. But some Roman dishes, for example stewed flamingoes, would now be considered most unusual!

Some small birds were eaten.

Mealtimes

The main meal of the day was in the late afternoon or early evening. At other times, people ate snacks to keep them going. Hot food was often bought at street stalls – particularly by those living in apartments, which often had no kitchens because of the danger of fire.

What did they eat?

Most meals were based on foods such as bread, lentils, beans, vegetables, fruit and a little meat or fish. They used a lot of olive oil, and honey to sweeten foods. The Romans ate small birds, and another favourite meal was dormouse served with honey and poppy seeds. People used a powerful fish sauce called *garum*, which was made from fish guts seasoned and left to mature in the sun for 4–6 weeks.

Slaves were given only a rough porridge, and there were handouts of bread or grain for the poor.

Did You Know?

Many foods we enjoy today were not known to the Romans. They had no tomatoes, potatoes, chocolate, oranges, pasta, coffee, tea or sugar.

This mosaic shows grapes. Grapes were enjoyed as a fruit and used to make juice and wine.

A jug made from glass

And something to drink?

Romans drank wine, diluted with water and sometimes sweetened with honey. They collected water from public fountains. People also drank milk – especially goat's milk – as well as grape juice.

A bowl and spoons made from bone. These were found at Pompeii.

A selection of Roman dishes

Fried snails in fennel sauce

Roast pork with celery seeds

Spiced seafood dumplings

Sea urchins cooked in wine

Lamb in coriander and onion sauce

Eggs with almond sauce

Peas with sausage and calf's brains

Fish stewed in seasoned wine

Honey omelette

Cinnamon sweet cakes

A Roman feast

The main meal of the day could last for hours and turn into a party. These parties were often fun, but sometimes guests would discuss subjects such as politics.

The guests arrive

Guests arrived for dinner parties in the early evening. They left their sandals by the door and were announced by an usher who showed them to their places.

The Romans liked to eat lying on couches. Three people could rest on each couch, and the couches were arranged on three sides of a table. Children sat on stools at the end of the dining room.

Top Facts

- Each couch had a head and a foot, and the most important person on each couch sat at the head.

- People ate from serving dishes; they did not generally use individual plates.

Did You Know?

Greedy diners would sometimes make themselves sick so they could eat even more, but many people thought this was disgusting.

Time to eat

People ate with their hands most of the time. Guests were offered bowls of perfumed water to wash their hands between courses, and each person had a napkin.

There might be as many as seven courses. Parties were a chance to show how much money you had, and some dishes were very elaborate. One writer describes a roast boar stuffed with live thrushes, which flew out when the boar was carved.

Dancing
This painting shows slaves dancing to entertain their masters.

Entertainment

The Romans liked to be entertained with music and acrobatics while they ate. When people had finished eating there was often more entertainment – perhaps clowns or dancing girls. Sometimes there were even drinking competitions, where people had to empty their cups in a single gulp!

Music

The Romans used a variety of stringed instruments, such as the lyre shown in this wall painting. They also had wind instruments as well as drums, cymbals and castanets.

Going to the baths

Most Roman houses had no bathrooms, so people went to bathhouses. But going to the baths was about more than simply getting clean.

Public bathing

Every Roman town and city had baths, and so did the forts. Baths were a place where you could meet your friends and relax after the day's work as well as bathe. You could exercise or play board games. Women either had their own bathhouses or went to public baths in the morning, when the men weren't there.

Inside a bathhouse

Bathers went into a series of rooms, each hotter than the last. These hot rooms could be steamy or dry. This made bathers sweat, opening their pores and cleaning their skin. Slaves rubbed olive oil on them and then scraped it off, together with any dirt, using a long curved stick called a *strigil*. Afterwards, bathers jumped in a tepid bath and then swam in a cold pool. The visit finished with a massage.

Top Facts

- All baths had the same areas. They were the *caldarium*, the hot rooms; the *tepidarium*, the warm pool; and the *frigidarium*, the cold pool.

- The biggest public baths, built in Rome by the emperor Caracalla in AD 219, held 1600 people.

Did You Know?

People used the baths as a club, where they knew they could meet their friends. They could also buy drinks and snacks, chat or gamble. The baths usually closed at sunset.

The entrance to the public baths at Herculaneum, near Pompeii

The remains of the Roman baths in the town of Bath, England

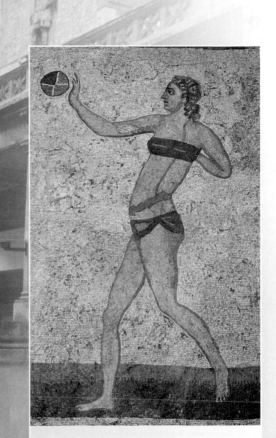

Exercise

Bathers often began by doing some exercise – like the woman in this mosaic from the floor of a bathhouse in Sicily.

Plan of a typical Roman bathhouse

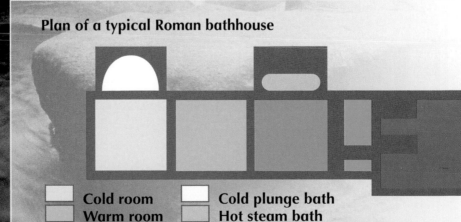

Cold room	Cold plunge bath
Warm room	Hot steam bath
Hot room	Hot water tank
	Furnace room

Chariots and the Games

The Romans enjoyed chariot races, held at racetracks. They also liked going to the amphitheatre to watch bloodthirsty shows called the Games.

Going to the races

The huge Circus Maximus in Rome was the greatest racetrack in the empire. It could seat more than a quarter of a million people.

Most races were for chariots pulled by four horses. The drivers and chariots belonged to one of four teams – the Whites, Reds, Blues and Greens. Each team had supporters, like football teams today. People could lose lots of money gambling on their favourites. Chariot racing was fast and dangerous and there were frequent crashes, especially when the chariots turned at the end of the track.

Did You Know?
A chariot could still win a race if it had lost its driver, as long as it crossed the line first.

A mosaic showing
Roman charioteers

The Colosseum

The Games took place in amphitheatres, large open-air
arenas surrounded with seats. Amphitheatres were built all
over the empire. The biggest was the Flavian Amphitheatre
in Rome, known as the Colosseum. The Colosseum was the
tallest building in Rome and could hold more than 50,000
people. The Games that opened it in AD 80 lasted 100 days.

Animal fights

Wild animals, such as lions and panthers, fought each other or
were hunted by animal fighters called *bestiarii*. Sometimes animals
were used to kill convicted criminals, too.

Gladiators

Most Romans enjoyed gladiator fights. All over the empire, crowds watched specially trained men fight each other – often to the death.

Fighters

In the early days, gladiators were slaves, prisoners of war or criminals. Later some free men actually volunteered, and many people thought that being a gladiator was glamorous. Some became very famous. There were special gladiator schools, which were very tough. Novices learned to fight with wooden swords and shields.

Gladiators at the Games

Gladiator fights were an important part of the Games, and the biggest ones were held in Rome. These festivals could last for weeks. Gladiators entered the arena and marched round it in a procession, then paired off and began fighting. Bets were placed on the results.

Did You Know?

There are records of female gladiators in the arena. They fought wild beasts or each other, not men, and there were far fewer of them. Female gladiators were banned after AD 200.

Underground

Underneath the floor of an amphitheatre was a maze of tunnels and rooms. We can see these today at the Colosseum in Rome because the original floor has not survived. Fighters waited here, and it was also where animals were kept for the wild beast games.

The contest

A fight lasted until one gladiator either was badly wounded or surrendered, then a trumpet would sound. The loser appealed for mercy to the emperor, who took his cue from the crowd. If the fight had been good, the gladiator was likely to be spared. If it had been bad, or if the fighter was unpopular, he would be killed.

A mosaic showing a fight against a panther

Top Facts

- Not all Romans enjoyed the bloodthirsty shows. The emperor Marcus Aurelius used to write letters during fights instead of watching.

- Gladiators had a special dinner the night before a contest, though some may not have felt much like eating.

Equipment

Gladiators used a variety of different weapons and armour. This actor, dressed as a Roman gladiator, is wearing a leather mask, which protects his nose and mouth but still allows him to see well.

The end of empire

The Roman Empire seemed as though it would last forever. But things gradually began to go wrong – several emperors were killed or removed by the army, the frontiers were attacked, and famine and plague killed many people. By the middle of the second century AD the mighty empire had started to fall apart.

Dividing the empire

Diocletian became emperor in AD 284. He decided that the empire was too big for one person to control and split it in two. He ruled the eastern half and appointed another general, Maximian, to rule the west. They both retired in AD 305 and a struggle for power began.

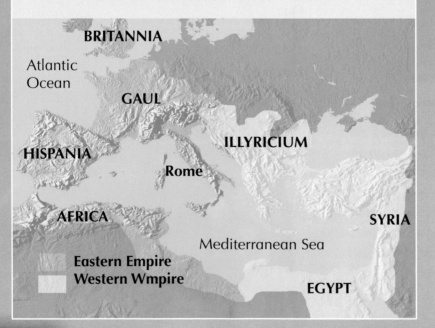

BRITANNIA

Atlantic Ocean

GAUL

HISPANIA

ILLYRICIUM

Rome

AFRICA

SYRIA

Mediterranean Sea

Eastern Empire
Western Wmpire

EGYPT

Constantine

Constantine was declared emperor by the army at York in AD 306. In 312 he defeated his main rival Maxentius. Constantine ruled both parts of the empire, though he was based in the east. He allowed Christians to worship; they had previously been punished.

The fall of Rome

In AD 395 the Empire split once more. The western half was soon attacked by barbarian tribes from the north-east. They invaded the city of Rome in 410, then ransacked it again in 455. The last emperor, Romulus Augustus, was forced into exile in AD 476. Rome had fallen.

A ruined Roman temple. The gilded roof tiles on the temples were taken by the attackers.

Eastern Empire

Justinian (AD 527–65) ruled the Eastern Empire. By this time the empire in the west had been destroyed. The empire in the east survived and became known as the Byzantine Empire.

The ruins of the Roman theatre at Leptis Magna, North Africa. Leptis Magna was part of the Western Empire.

ASIA, THE AMERICAS AND AUSTRALIA

Though Egypt, Greece and Rome are the best-known ancient civilizations, others grew all over the world. Some, in the Middle East and Mesopotamia, saw the earliest beginnings of farming or writing, and the first towns. Some left spectacular monuments, such as the Great Wall of China or the great Mayan cities and temples in Central America. Some had always been known – the Persian Empire, for example – while others, such as the Indus Valley Civilization, were forgotten until they were discovered by archaeologists at the beginning of the 20th century.

The first farmers and towns

For hundreds of thousands of years people lived in small groups, hunting animals and collecting wild plants. The beginning of farming allowed people to live more settled lives.

Slow changes

The first farmers lived about 12,000 years ago in the Middle East. People had gathered grass seeds and used them as food for many years. Then they began sowing some of these seeds in the ground and harvesting them when ripe. Slowly the plants changed as people chose only the best ones with the fattest grains.

Top Facts

- The fat grains of the new breeds of grasses, early types of wheat and barley, were ground between two stones, producing flour for making bread.

- People living in Jericho stored wild wheat and barley as much as 12,500 years ago!

The remains of one of the first towns, Catalhöyük in modern Turkey

Keeping animals

As well as planting seeds, people began to tame and raise young animals. They bred from the most useful ones and, over time, these 'domestic' animals became much easier to handle than their wild ancestors. People still hunted for some of their food. Dogs, which may have been bred from wolves, were useful in hunting.

Did You Know?
The houses in Catalhöyük were made of mud bricks. People entered them through a trap door in the roof and went down a ladder into the main room.

Settling down

Having a dependable source of food meant people didn't need to move about so much in order to gather enough to eat. They could stay longer in one place and build permanant settlements and homes. Places such as Jericho, by the River Jordan, and Catalhöyük in Turkey became permanant villages and grew into towns. By 8000 BC Jericho had solid walls surrounding it and people lived there all year round.

The skulls of Jericho

Human skulls, covered in plaster and decorated, were found under some floors in Jericho. Perhaps they were ancestors, put there to protect the house.

Mesopotamia and the first cities

From about 5500 BC, settlements grew up in Mesopotamia, the land between the Tigris and Euphrates rivers. People there made many important inventions, and these inventions had a great effect on civilizations across the world.

Changing the land

The flat land between the two rivers was dry and rain was unreliable. But the rivers flooded regularly and farmers created systems of pools and channels to trap floodwater so that they could water their crops. Soon people could grow more than they could eat and were able to trade their produce for other goods.

The first city

By about 3500 BC some villages were beginning to grow into cities. The first one was Uruk, in the southern part of Mesopotamia (often called Sumer). By about 3000 BC almost 50,000 people lived there. There were large public buildings and massive temples – and the city was surrounded by a wall.

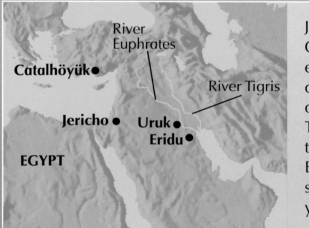

Jericho and Catalhöyük are the earliest towns discovered by archaeologists. The Mesopotamian towns of Uruk and Eridu followed several thousand years later.

Top Facts

- The name 'Mesopotamia' comes from a Greek word meaning 'between two rivers'.

- The city of Uruk appears in the Bible, where it is called Erech. Its temples could have been seen from a long way away.

Did You Know?

The White Temple at Uruk was built on a high platform. A leopard and a lion cub had been buried in the temple's foundations by its builders, maybe as a sacrifice to the gods.

Early inventions

As farming became more organized, fewer people were needed in the fields, so they could do other things such as make pots, jewellery, weapons and other objects. The Mesopotamians created the first potter's wheel. The first vehicles with wheels were invented there too – these were carts pulled by donkeys.

Clay writing tablet

The ruins of Uruk

Writing tablets

It may have been the temple staff who developed the most important Mesopotamian invention: writing. These Mesopotamians were the first scribes. More than 5000 tablets with early writing on them have been found at Uruk.

Paying the priests

The farmers and people who lived at Uruk had to give some of their produce to the temples. Part went to feed the temple staff and priests and the rest was stored for the city.

Statue of a priest from Sumeria

Keeping records

Writing made it possible for people to keep records, and these records have taught us many things about people from the distant past.

How did scribes write?

Small tablets of soft clay were smoothed off and marks made on them using a piece of sharpened wood or ivory called a stylus. Once the clay dried, the records were permanent. At first scribes drew pictures of what they were recording, known as pictographs. So grain was shown as an ear of wheat, for example. They had a system of marks for numbers as well.

Pictograms

Making writing simpler

Over time, pictographs were made simpler. Some symbols came to mean sounds. This meant that several could be used together to make a word for something that couldn't be shown as a picture. Others were used together to show an idea – like a head and a bowl, which meant 'to eat'. The simpler signs were made with the end of the writing tool, which looked like a wedge, as shown here. This writing is called cuneiform, which means 'wedge shaped'.

A cylinder seal

Signing your work

Small round seals, called cylinder seals, were used to 'sign' clay tablets. This showed they had been written, or authorized, by the person who had rolled their seal over the damp clay. Many of the seals have pictures of animals or people on them as well as their owner's name. The cylinder seal of Idi-Ilum is shown on the right. You can see the image produced by the seal above.

Writing across the world

Different ways of writing developed independently in other places. The first writing in China was scratched on bones with sharp tools. The Maya, in Central America, engraved their symbols on stone.

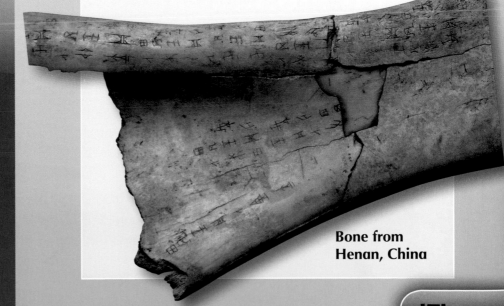

Bone from Henan, China

Top Facts

- Cuneiform symbols were used to write many different languages.

- Cuneiform was still in use up to the time of Jesus, but was then forgotten completely. Experts worked out how to read it again in the 1800s.

Cities of Sumer

By about 3500 BC some of the towns in the southern part of Mesopotamia, an area called Sumer, had grown into cities where thousands of people lived. The larger cities, such as Ur, Kish and Babylon, were capitals of small kingdoms – and these kingdoms were often at war.

City states

Each city had its own ruler who also controlled the farmland and smaller settlements that lay around the city, so that many small states were formed. The different city states often fought about land and water supplies.

Inside the first cities

Most cities were surrounded by walls and the buildings were usually made of mud bricks. In the middle was the temple and the royal palace. Homes and workshops surrounded the official buildings, and there was also a marketplace. Houses were built side by side, along winding streets.

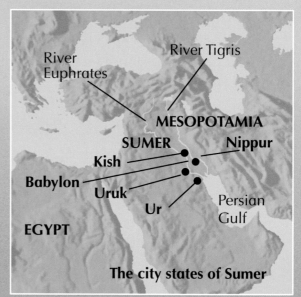

The city states of Sumer

The ziggurat of Nanna at Ur

Temples

Each city had its own god. In the early days, the god's temple was built on a platform to raise it higher than other buildings. Eventually newer temples were built on top of the rubble of older ones. There could be several levels, all linked by stairs, with the shrine of the god on the top. These huge stepped temples are called ziggurats.

Everyday life

Many people worked for the temple. Inside its walls were storerooms and workshops. Scribes worked there, too, and many records have survived. Craftspeople created beautiful things for the temples, such as these stone statues of men praying. Trade grew and ships sailed along the rivers, carrying fine cloth to other lands and bringing back precious goods such as ivory.

Top Facts

- Enlil was the overall ruler of the Sumerian gods and his temple at Nippur was the most important holy place.

- People often buried their dead under the plaster floors of their houses.

The tombs of the kings of Ur

Ur was an important Sumerian city state. The treasures discovered there by the archaeologist Leonard Wooley in the 1920s showed that Ur was also a very wealthy city.

The graveyard

In about 2600 BC the people of the city of Ur began to use a graveyard to bury their dead. Almost all the graves that Leonard Wooley found were simple and belonged to ordinary people, but some were larger with underground rooms. Although most of these larger tombs had been robbed, Wooley found two that had not been touched at all.

The steps of the ziggurat, or temple mound, at Ur

A dagger and sheath found in the tomb

Royal tombs and treasures

The two untouched tombs discovered by Leonard Wooley belonged to kings who ruled Ur around 2500 BC. Inside, Wooley found amazing treasure including weapons such as the dagger and sheath above, armour, necklaces of precious stones and gold, musical instruments, headdresses and a game box. A lot of the materials used to make these things had come from faraway places, as distant as Afghanistan.

Human sacrifices

The tombs also contained human remains. Many of the palace servants had died with their kings. There were even animals – the oxen who had dragged wagons down into the tomb. In the largest tomb, known as the Death Pit, there were the bodies of nearly 70 women and six men. The bodies lay in neat rows and there was no sign of struggle. It looks as though the victims may have taken poison.

Did You Know?

People may have been drugged before going down into the tombs to die. We think it must have been terrible, but it may have been thought a great honour for servants to be chosen to enter the afterlife with their masters.

Musical instruments

Musicians were among the people who died in the royal tombs. We know this because they were found with the remains of their instruments. Although the wood had rotted away, it has been possible to work out what the instruments looked like. Many objects have been rebuilt, such as the lyre shown above. It is decorated with a bull's head made from gold and a precious blue stone called lapis lazuli.

Empires of Mesopotamia

Ur was the centre of an early empire. It was at its most important in about 2000 BC, 500 years after the royal tombs were sealed. But there were other empires at this time.

King Sargon

The first empire in the area was created by Sargon, who was the ruler of Akkad, north of Sumer, in about 2300 BC. He conquered lands between the Mediterranean and the Persian Gulf, including Sumer, but his successors could not hold them. His empire fell apart about 2230 BC.

Many Archaeologists think this is a sculpture of Sargon

Ur rises again

In about 2000 BC Ur-Nammu, the king of Ur, and his son Shulgi were able to control areas up the River Tigris and parts of Iran. They had a strong army and a well organized system of government. The kings became rich – receiving food and goods from the farmers and craftsmen they ruled over. They built large palaces and temples.

Babylon

The city state of Babylon had been controlled by Ur, but it became independent when Ur's empire collapsed. Babylon's sixth ruler, Hammurabi, came to the throne in 1792 BC. He was a great soldier and conquered both Sumer and Akkad. During his reign Babylon grew rich but, shortly after Hammurabi died in 1750 BC, his state of Babylon collapsed.

Did You Know?

The famous Hanging Gardens of Babylon were created in about 600 BC by King Nebuchadnezzar II. Babylon was once again a powerful state and Nebuchadnezzar and his father had rebuilt Babylon, making it the most spectacular city in the region.

The Uphrates River – the city of Ur was built close to where the river meets the Persian Gulf.

Hammurabi's laws

Hammurabi made 282 laws, which covered many aspects of daily life. They were engraved on a tall stone. At the top, Hammurabi is shown receiving laws. They were tough, but gave women some status and rights over property.

The Assyrian Empire

The Assyrians originally lived in an area beside the River Tigris in northern Mesopotamia. They created not just one great empire, but two.

The first empire

The Assyrians began expanding westwards during the Bronze Age. They ruled the places they conquered firmly. But this early empire was attacked by nomads from the north and west. By 1030 BC they had retreated to their original home.

The great Assyrian Empire

A series of strong kings with powerful armies began pushing outwards again, and by 650 BC the Assyrian Empire stretched from the Persian Gulf to the Mediterranean and down into Egypt.

Did You Know?
The armies of the great Assyrian Empire were well trained and used iron weapons, which gave them an advantage over their enemies, who used softer bronze weapons.

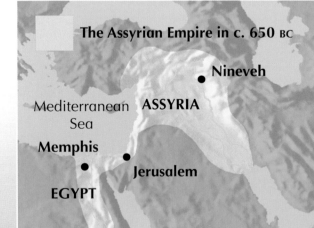

The Assyrian Empire in c. 650 BC

Nineveh

Mediterranean Sea

ASSYRIA

Memphis

Jerusalem

EGYPT

A modern illustration shows Assyrian soldiers using a battering ram to attack the fortress city of Samaria.

The army

Assyrian armies were feared by other people. Their foot soldiers were armed with spears and shields, and there were bowmen and men who used slingshots. There were also horsemen and chariots. The Assyrians attacked cities using battering rams and climbed city walls using ladders and ramps.

Assyrian rule

When the Assyrians captured a city they usually burnt it to the ground. Its people were either killed or sent to other parts of the empire. Many of these people were used as slaves to build huge palaces and temples for the Assyrian kings, and some had to join the Assyrian army. Eventually the conquered nations joined, to fight against the cruelty. The Assyrians were finally overthrown in 609 BC.

Cities of Assyria

The Assyrian conquests brought vast wealth. Great palaces and temples were built by the Assyrian emperors, and cities were rich.

Top Facts

- Several of the Assyrian kings had private zoos filled with exotic animals.

- Assyrian cities had a large enclosed area near the palace. It was where the soldiers and their commanders lived, and where weapons were stored.

Huge gates guarded the entrance to the ancient city of Nineveh.

The Assyrian city of Nimrud was built on the banks of the River Tigris. This modern illustration shows what it might have been like.

Capital cities

The capital of the Assyrian Empire was changed several times and the Assyrian kings built enormous monuments in each of their capitals. These cities were also large: about 100,000 people lived in Nineveh, which was capital between 705 and 612 BC. The cities were surrounded by high walls with huge gates. They had good water supplies and food was brought from all over the empire to feed their populations.

Palaces

Palaces were built in a part of the city surrounded by a wall. The area within the wall was the size of a small town and also included the city's main temples. People entered the palace through gates guarded by gigantic sculptures of winged bulls with human heads.

Inside the palace there were public rooms as well as private areas for the royal family, storerooms and workshops. The walls were decorated with carvings often showing the king at war, hunting or even enjoying his gardens. The temples were also lavishly decorated.

Libraries

Assyrian kings put together libraries – collections of writing on tablets. The clay tablets, like the one shown above, came from all parts of the empire and some were centuries old. They record historical events and were vital in helping modern scholars understand the ancient language of Sumer.

The Persian Empire

Two tribes, the Medes and the Persians, moved westwards from Central Asia and settled in what is now Iran in about 2000 BC. The Persians created one of the largest empires of the ancient world.

Powerful kings

Originally the Medes were the stronger of the two tribes, but the Persian ruler Cyrus II defeated them in 551 BC. He began to extend the area the Persians controlled, moving westwards to the Mediterranean and east towards Central Asia. His successor conquered Egypt. The next king, Darius, who is shown in this carving, came to the throne in 522 BC. He added Thrace to the Persian Empire.

Persepolis

Darius started building a new capital and a huge palace at Persepolis. The enormous buildings were put on top of a platform 15 metres high so they looked even more impressive.

Ruling the empire

The Persian emperors divided their lands into 20 provinces. Each one was ruled by a trusted governor. A system of roads was built between the provinces so that the emperor could communicate easily with the governors. The main royal road ran for about 2500 kilometres.

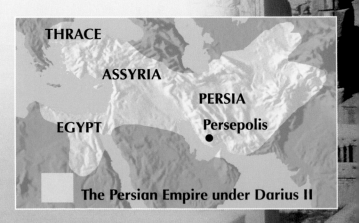

THRACE

ASSYRIA

PERSIA

EGYPT

Persepolis

The Persian Empire under Darius II

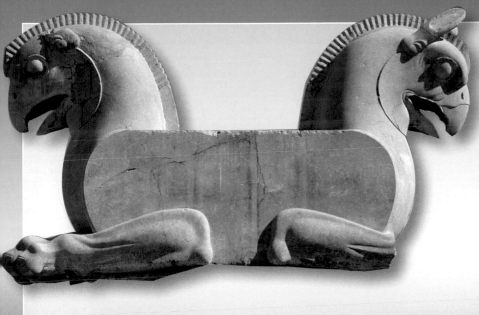

The Apadana

The Apadana was a gigantic hall at Persepolis where people were presented to the king. It had very tall columns topped with the heads of great animals. These made it look as though the ceiling was held up by giant bulls, lions or imaginary beasts such as the griffin shown here.

The ruins of Darius's capital city, Persepolis.

Defeat and destruction

The Persian Empire was finally overthrown by the Greek king Alexander the Great in 330 BC. This was the end for the great city of Persepolis too. The Persian king Xerxes had burnt the Greek city of Athens 150 years before and, in revenge, Alexander set fire to Persepolis.

The Indus Civilization

In about 2500 BC a major civilization grew in the lands around the River Indus in south-west Asia. It was huge – but it declined and was forgotten. It was only discovered again by archaeologists in the 1920s.

Towns and countryside

The Indus Civilization, as it was called, covered an enormous area. The rivers brought rich silt down from the mountains, which made the land perfect for farming. There were small settlements, villages, towns and five large cities. The biggest ones, Mohenjo-Daro and Harappa, had populations of about 40,000 people.

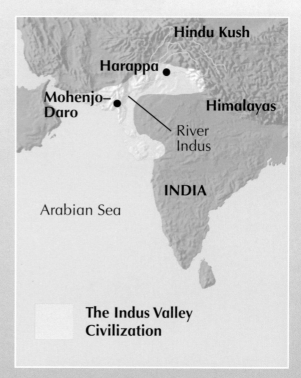

Hindu Kush

Harappa

Mohenjo–Daro

Himalayas

River Indus

INDIA

Arabian Sea

The Indus Valley Civilization

Archaeologists think this is a sculpture of a priest.

Who ruled the Indus Civilization?

Many things were the same across the Indus Civilization, such as the system of weights and measures. Some people think this meant the Indus people must have had a strong ruler, but no evidence has been found of palaces or any lavish burials or individual wealth. There may have been a ruling group of priests instead.

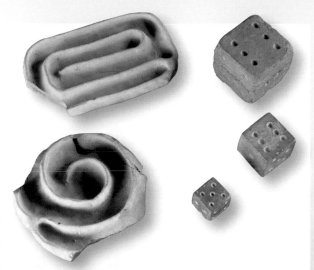

Everyday objects

Archaeologists working in the Indus settlements have found many beautiful objects, for example small statues, jewellery and even toys and games such as these maze games and dice.

Why were the cities abandoned?

The Indus Civilization grew for a thousand years and then ended. We don't know why. Perhaps the rivers dried up or changed course. Whatever it was, it seems to have been gradual rather than sudden.

Scholars think the Great Bath at Mohenjo-Daro was probably used during religious ceremonies.

Top Facts

• **The people of the Indus Civilization traded with the Mesopotamian states many kilometres to the north, sending them luxury goods such as ivory and semi-precious stones.**

• **Scholars have found examples of the writing of the Indus Civilization at Harappa, but nobody has yet been able to read it.**

Ancient China

At first, China consisted of many separate states, which became more united under the kings of the Shang and Zhou families. In 221 BC Qin Shi Huangdi became the most powerful emperor China had ever seen.

First rulers

In about 1700 BC, the rulers of the Shang Dynasty, or family, became the strongest kings. They controlled large areas of China for about 600 years. Shang kings kept tight control of their people and used many slaves.

In 1122 BC the Zhou Dynasty took over from the Shang and ruled for about 900 years. But this was a very unsettled period: there were many revolts and wars because the nobles from the small states that made up the empire grew strong enough to challenge the king. The states fought bitterly among themselves, and the empire was also invaded by people living to the north of China.

Top Facts

- The armour worn by Shang soldiers was made of wood and bamboo, heavily padded for extra protection.

- The Great Wall has been extended, repaired and maintained for over 2000 years.

ASIA

Great Wall

CHINA

Pacific Ocean

Indian Ocean

Did You Know?

The earliest Chinese writing was made up of pictures, which represented words rather than sounds. These pictures were gradually changed into the symbols used today.

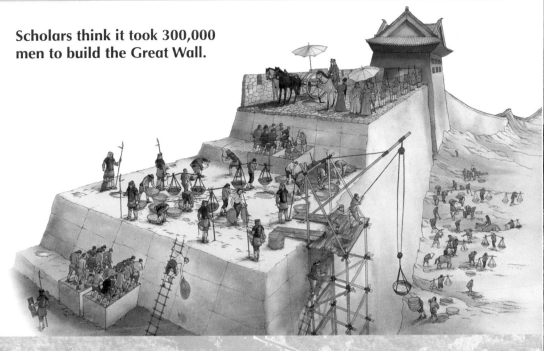

Scholars think it took 300,000 men to build the Great Wall.

Qin Shi Huangdi's Great Wall

During the wars, many states built walls to defend themselves. In 221 BC the ruler of the state of Qin finally won control and took the title Qin Shi Huangdi, meaning First Emperor. He began building a massive wall, designed to keep out his enemies, by joining lots of existing barriers. The wall was made from local materials – stones were used in mountain areas but if stone wasn't easy to find, earth was mounded up and compacted to form a sturdy wall.

Did You Know?

The Chinese discovered how to make silk from the cocoons of the silk worm. They used the silk fibres to make cloth and paper.

China's first emperor

The first emperor, Qin Shi Huangdi, began reforming the enormous areas he controlled. The empire became wealthy under him and grew under his successors.

Qin Shi Huangdi

The first emperor brought a single government to the whole of China. All across the country people used the same weights and measures, coins and writing. Huge projects, such as the Great Wall, were begun. The most amazing survival of Qin Shi's reign is his gigantic tomb.

The emperor's tomb

Qin Shi Huangdi wanted to live forever, but he died in 210 BC. Work on his tomb had begun years earlier. There is a great burial mound, which may still contain the body of the emperor himself. Around this artificial mountain are lots of different-sized pits. In these, the archaeologists found a whole army made of terracotta – a type of clay.

The soldiers are large – most are between 180 and 190 centimetres tall.

The Terracotta Army

The emperor had an army of thousands of men made. There were soldiers, archers, and even horses. There are 7000 soldiers and each one has a different face. There are archers, foot soldiers, crossbowmen, charioteers, two generals and many others. All the details of their armour are shown. The soldiers originally had real weapons, but most of these were stolen after the emperor died.

Top Facts

- **The first soldiers of the terracotta army were discovered by local people digging a well in 1974.**

- **The soldiers were originally painted in bright colours and traces of paint remain on some of them.**

The Han emperors

Soon after Qin Shi Huangdi died, the Han Dynasty began. The Chinese empire grew under the Han emperors, who ruled with the help of officials called mandarins. Some burials of Han nobles have been found. In one, Prince Liu Sheng and his wife were buried in suits made of small pieces of jade held together with gold wire.

Prince Liu Sheng

Great Zimbabwe

Some of the biggest ruins in Africa are at Great Zimbabwe, where huge stone walls still reach up into the sky.

Capital of a Shona empire

The first people who lived at Great Zimbabwe, from AD 500–900, were a few farmers who didn't use stone. The ancestors of the Shona people arrived and started building in about 1270. Great Zimbabwe grew and grew, until there were about 18,000 people living there. They traded far and wide until about 1450.

Stone buildings

There are two collections of massive stone ruins. Between them were many smaller clay houses where ordinary people lived. On the hill above were lots of stone buildings where the ruler lived with some of his family. Important officials probably lived up there too, and maybe some priests.

Top Facts

- The people from Great Zimbabwe used trading towns on the coast, and pieces of Chinese and Persian pottery have been found.

- The ruler needed to be sure that he could feed his people all year round. There are stone bins in the valley for storing grain.

Where it happened

Great Zimbabwe was the centre of an empire that stretched from northern South Africa up to the Zambesi river, and from eastern Botswana to western Mozambique. It traded through towns on the African coast of the Indian Ocean.

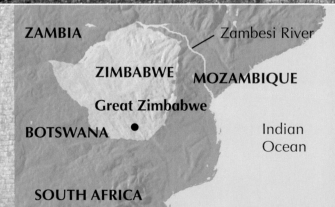

ZAMBIA

Zambesi River

ZIMBABWE MOZAMBIQUE

Great Zimbabwe

BOTSWANA ●

Indian Ocean

SOUTH AFRICA

The Great Enclosure

There is also another collection of stone buildings in the valley. They are inside a huge stone wall called the Great Enclosure, which is 244 metres long, 5 metres wide and 10–11 metres tall – and which uses about 900,000 stone blocks. Inside, among other things, is a stone tower, which is about 9 metres tall.

Tower

Did You Know?

Great Zimbabwe was built on the Zimbabwe Plateau. The plateau's height meant that the settlement was not infested by the tsetse flies that could spread disease among people and cattle.

The birds

Seven stone posts were found in the area of the palace up on the hill. Another was found in the valley ruins. Each one was topped with a stone figure that looks like a mixture of a bird and a human. One of these birds is shown on the flag of Zimbabwe.

The Great Enclosure

The Americas

During the last Ice Age, which began about 100,000 years ago, the pattern of land and sea was very different. Changes in the climate led people from Asia to explore further afield in search of food.

Land bridges and canoes

At this time, groups of hunters followed herds of reindeer, musk ox and mammoths. As the weather warmed up these animals moved further north. So did their hunters.

There was land, linking Siberia and Alaska, that is now under the sea, and this is probably how the first people arrived in North America. Others may have followed the coastline in canoes. There are traces of early settlements in places as far apart as Alaska, Brazil and Chile. As the climate warmed even more, ice melted, sea levels rose and Asia and North America were separated.

Rock art at Canyonlands National Park in Utah, USA

Top facts

- Traces of tents called tepees have been found from nearly 5000 years ago. All that is left are the stones that held down the skin walls.

- Early hunters in North America followed the herds of animals on foot. Horses were introduced by the Spanish in the 1500s.

Arctic Ocean

Asia

Siberia

Alsaka

North America

Pacific Ocean

This map shows the continents after the land between Asia and North America was submerged.

Spear points

North America

Most of the large animals that had lived during the Ice Age, such as the mammoth, had died out, but there were other herds. People now hunted bison and caribou, and some relied on fishing. The hunters made stone tools. In some places this way of life lasted until the 1800s.

Moundbuilders

Some groups of people began to build enclosures and mounds during the first century BC. The tradition lasted for hundreds of years but little is known about why they were built. Sometimes there were buildings on the mounds, and sometimes they contained graves. Often they were just gigantic mounds of earth. The Great Serpent Mound (above) in Ohio is a long, winding, snake-shaped mound.

Chaco Canyon

The deserts of south-western America were difficult places in which to live. Some extraordinary ruins have been found at Chaco Canyon and Mesa Verde. They have survived very well in the dry desert air.

Farming and settling down

About 2500–2000 years ago people began growing maize, beans and squashes on the Colorado Plateau. They dug channels to allow water to reach their fields and became expert farmers.

In about AD 800, things changed again. Small farms were replaced by much bigger settlements built of stone. Some are enormous buildings, which archaeologists have called 'great houses'.

Top facts

• The people who lived in places such as Chaco Canyon are often called the Pueblo peoples. *'Pueblo'* means village or town in Spanish, the language that was introduced by the Spanish settlers in the 1500s.

• The settlements in Chaco were thriving – and then building suddenly stopped in the middle of the 1100s.

North America

Mesa Verde ●

Colorado

Chaco Canyon ●

New Mexico

We can still see the painted pattern on this wooden headdress found at Chaco Canyon.

Chaco Canyon

There are several great houses in Chaco Canyon, New Mexico. Pueblo Bonito, shown here, is the largest with over 600 rooms. It was five or six storeys high. Building the great houses must have involved lots of people. The ones in Chaco Canyon, for instance, would have needed 200,000 wooden beams, which had to be brought from several kilometres away.

We still don't really know what most of the buildings were for. People may have lived there, or they could have been temples. People were buried in some rooms at Pueblo Bonito. There were also round structures called *kivas*, which could have been meeting places.

Did You Know?

The 14 people who were buried in one room at Pueblo Bonito were accompanied by thousands of shell decorations – and by 56,000 pieces of the precious stone turquoise.

The mystery of Mesa Verde

The settlements at Mesa Verde in Colorado, north of Chaco Canyon, are spectacular. They are mysterious, too, because we don't know why they were abandoned in the 1200s.

Under the cliffs

The most dramatic ruins are the cliff settlements. They are tucked under the top of the cliff along the edges of steep valleys. The buildings are packed closely together and often linked to each other. Some buildings have towers, and there are also round buildings called *kivas*.

The cliff settlements are like large villages and were often built in places that could be easily defended. Steps led up the rock to the fields, which were on the plateau above.

Top facts

- Many everyday items have been found. Sandals discovered at Mesa Verde were made from yucca plants.

- There are 150 rooms in the cliff palace at Mesa Verde. The buildings are made from stone, wood and plaster.

Pottery

Much of the pottery found at Mesa Verde is decorated with black and white patterns.

Violence!

Skeletons have been found at Mesa Verde with arrow wounds or damage from heavy blows. Archaeologists think there had always been some violence there. But by the 1100s there were many more killings, and by the 1200s the settlements had been abandoned.

What happened?

Nobody knows for sure why people stopped living at places like Chaco Canyon and Mesa Verde. Some archaeologists think it was because there had been too many people, and that they had cut down all the trees and exhausted the soil. That would have made farming almost impossible and might have led to fighting. Others think that droughts or periods of cold weather could have made farming too difficult. There are many theories, but we will probably never know for sure.

Early kingdoms in the Andes

Civilizations began appearing in the Andes Mountains of South America in about 800 BC. They left behind them some beautiful and mysterious things.

The Moche

The Moche were powerful rulers of the northern Andes from AD 100–800. They built ceremonial centres in river valleys where they constructed enormous temple pyramids. The rulers were rich and their people were skilled at many crafts, especially pottery. They also made many objects from gold and precious stones.

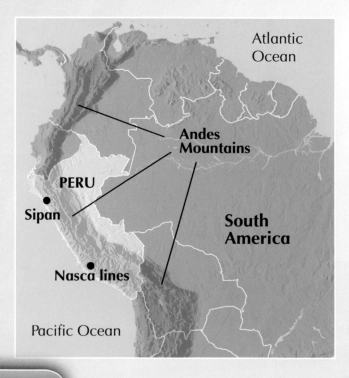

The Lord of Sipan

Several Moche royal tombs have been found at Sipan. In the middle of the first one was a coffin containing the body of a man. The coffin was also filled with precious objects such as gold and feather headdresses, royal banners, clothing decorated with gold and silver beads and the mask shown below.

Top Facts

- Moche temples were built from mud bricks. The biggest is thought to have taken 125 million bricks – and each one had to be carried into position.

- The Nasca had systems for bringing water from underground rivers to the surface, where it could be used. Some of these systems are still in use today.

Did You Know?

The tombs of Sipan were found by tomb robbers in 1987. There was so much gold that they quarrelled about it and one of them went to the police.

These Nasca lines, seen from above, are in the shape of a monkey.

Nasca

The Nasca people lived at about the same time as the Moche, but further south. They left some unique 'monuments' called the Nasca lines. The Nasca created thousands of straight lines and patterns on the desert floor by scraping away the surface to show the paler ground underneath. The patterns are so large that they cannot be fully seen from the ground. It has been suggested that groups of people walked along the lines of the patterns during religious ceremonies. Many of the shapes seem to be linked with the Sun and the position of water sources.

The lines on the right are in the shape of a spider

The Incas

The Inca Empire was the largest in the Americas. It covered most of what are now the countries of Peru, Bolivia, Ecuador and Chile.

Many kingdoms

The kingdom of Cuzco was the centre of the Inca Empire, which began in about AD 900. The Incas eventually conquered hundreds of different kingdoms and became lords over a huge area stretching for over 4000 kilometres.

Ruling the empire

The empire included many different peoples speaking many different languages, though the Inca language was used by officials everywhere. People were strictly controlled and had to pay taxes by working or giving things to the state. If they were rebellious, they were moved somewhere where they were surrounded by strangers who couldn't understand what they said.

Top Facts

- The Inca roads were narrow. They didn't have to be wide because there were no wheeled vehicles. Llamas or people were used to carry goods.

- Inca buildings are so strong that many have survived earthquakes that destroyed more modern structures.

Did You Know?

One of the most breathtaking Inca sites is the city of Machu Picchu. It was built high up on a mountain ridge in the Andes. It was a summer capital – a place the royal family could go to when it was too hot in Cuzco.

Machu Picchu

The ruins of the city of Machu Picchu

Inca roads

The Incas created a network of roads to link the places they ruled. These roads connected with smaller tracks and pathways, and ran all over the empire. Hostels and warehouses were built along the roads and messages were sent from place to place by official runners.

Master builders

The Incas were astonishing builders. They even changed the landscape by building terraces on mountain sides. They built with stone blocks, some of which were enormous. The blocks were moved into position using levers, rollers and pulleys, and they fitted together perfectly without mortar to keep them in place.

End of the empire

In 1532, Spanish soldiers under the command of the explorer Pizzaro arrived in Peru. Less than a year later the Inca emperor Atahualpa had been executed and the Inca empire had collapsed.

The Maya

In the 1900s, explorers John Stephens and Frederick Catherwood reported finding 'lost cities' in the jungles in parts of Central America. These cities belonged to the Maya civilization.

A carving of King Jaguar-bird

Cities and temples

The Maya seem to have started to build cities in about 300 BC. They were political and religious centres where many leaders and priests lived. Most ordinary people lived in the countryside around the cities.

Each city had a main area containing temples, the palace of the king and the homes of important nobles. There were also big public squares. Temples were often pyramid-shaped. These buildings were decorated with carvings of people or animals, and mysterious symbols.

The temple at Tikal in Guatamala

The pyramid at the Maya city of Chichen Itza

Peaceful people?

At first, archaeologists thought the Maya had been peaceful because their cities had no walls to protect them. Then scholars managed to read the symbols carved on the temples. The inscriptions showed that each city was the centre of a separate kingdom. There were many battles between them, and people were captured and sacrificed.

The ball game

The Maya played a ball game on the courtyards near their temples. A hard rubber ball had to be struck to the end of the ball court (or put through a hoop set in the wall) using parts of the body, such as the elbow or the thigh. Players were not allowed to use their hands or feet – and losers could be sacrificed to the gods.

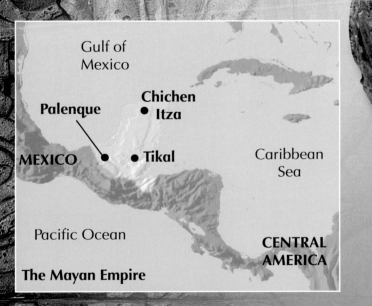

Gulf of Mexico

Palenque

Chichen
● Itza

MEXICO   ● Tikal

Caribbean
Sea

Pacific Ocean

CENTRAL
AMERICA

The Mayan Empire

Ball game hoop

203

Maya life

Kings and lords ruled Maya cities, supported by farmers who worked the land nearby.

Godly kings

Kings were important in Maya religion. They took the place of the gods in religious ceremonies and some even became gods after death. The kings were also thought to be responsible for the success of the harvest.

Powerful lords

Mayan lords were often relatives of the king. The lords were powerful and had large homes, but they had to serve the king. They led armies in war, collected taxes and organized building projects. Women could sometimes hold important positions, too.

The Jaguar Throne

The jaguar throne was found in the city of Chichen Itza. Mayan kings wanted to be associated with the powerful jaguar.

Top Facts

- Metal was very precious. Gold objects were often given to the gods. Sometimes they were thrown into sacred lakes.

- The Maya thought caves were gateways to the spirit world and many were religious shrines. One has over 100 paintings on the walls – 2 kilometres below the surface.

Did You Know?

The Maya built temples on top of their pyramids. They were not places for burials like Egyptian pyramids, except for one, at Palenque. Archaeologists lifted a slab there and found a staircase going to a huge room. Inside was an enormous tomb, which contained the remains of Pakal, Palenque's most important king.

The people

Most of the Maya were farmers. They grew maize, squashes, beans, root vegetables and chillies. They had to pay taxes to the king, either by working for him or by giving him some of their produce. Farming was hard work for the Maya because they had no metal tools or animals to drag ploughs. The Maya had not invented the wheel, so moving food was also difficult.

This painting on the wall of a tomb at Bonampak shows Mayan musicians.

What happened to the Maya?

Sometime in the 800s people left the Mayan cities and official histories stopped. In some places the change happened slowly, but in others it seems to have been sudden. There may have been too many people for the land to support, or droughts or fighting. When the Spanish arrived in 1524, Palenque (shown above) and the other main settlements had already been abandoned.

The Aztecs

The Aztecs originally lived in Mexico's northern deserts, and moved south into what is now Central America in the 1200s. They became powerful, and by the 1400s they had conquered large parts of Central America.

Tenochtitlan

The main Aztec city was Tenochtitlan, which was founded in about AD 1325. The city and the surrounding settlements grew very large. When the Spanish arrived in 1519 there were about one million people living there. The main part of Tenochtitlan was built in the middle of Lake Texcoco on an artificial island made by the Aztecs themselves.

Top Facts

- The Spanish destroyed most of Tenochtitlan, so we have to rely on their descriptions of what is was like. Anything left is now buried underneath Mexico City.

- The main temple at Tenochtitlan was dedicated to Tlaloc, the rain god, and Huitzilopochtli, the sun god.

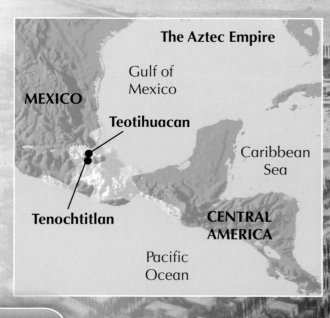

The Aztec Empire

MEXICO

Gulf of Mexico

Teotihuacan

Caribbean Sea

Tenochtitlan

CENTRAL AMERICA

Pacific Ocean

Did You Know?

The Aztecs relied on farming, but also used many wild plants. They made cakes from a tiny plant skimmed off the surface of the lake.

The city on the lake

The king's palace was on the island, but many ordinary people lived there, too. Most of the houses were only one storey high and the streets were laid out in a grid pattern. The city was divided into about 20 districts, connected by streets and canals. Food for the city was grown on floating gardens called *chinampas*. The *chinampas* were fertile and farmers used the water from the canals to water their crops. The main island was linked to the shore by roads built over the water.

This illustration shows what Tenochtitlan might have looked like.

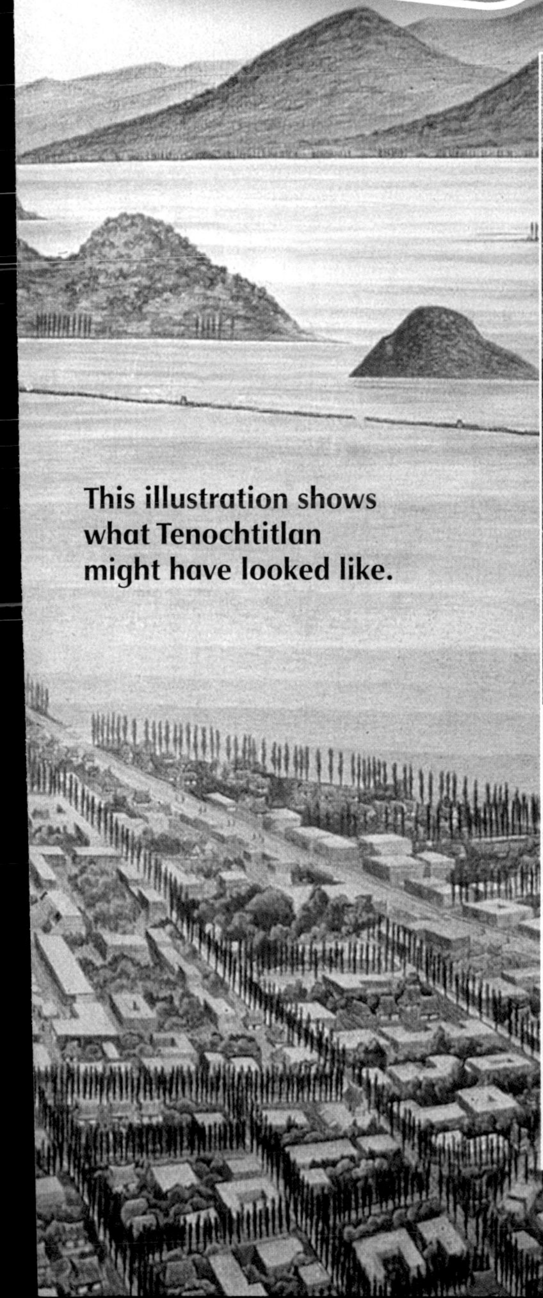

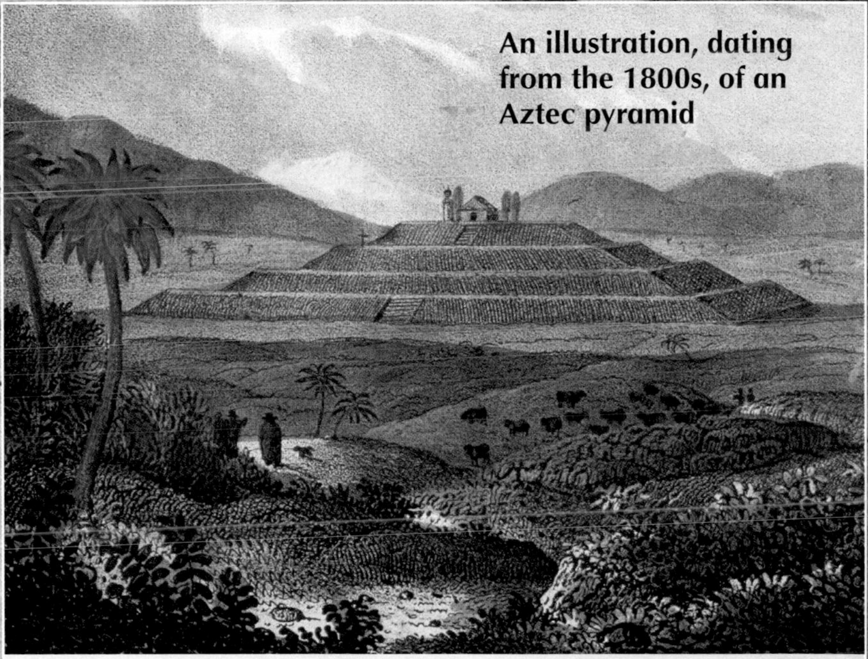

An illustration, dating from the 1800s, of an Aztec pyramid

Temples and palaces

In the middle of the city there were many important buildings. The Great Temple was shaped like a huge stepped pyramid. There were two shrines on the top. The king's palace was nearby. It had hundreds of rooms and courtyards on several levels, but the king only lived in those at the top. The rest were libraries, weapons stores and council rooms. There were also workshops and the royal kitchens. Every day, hundreds of nobles and court officials visited the palace to see the king.

Teotihuacan

The great city of Teotihuacan in Mexico was built about AD 300. We do not know who founded it but historians agree that the city was most important between AD 300 and AD 600. The Aztecs, who moved there 1000 years after it was built, gave the city the name Teotihuacan, which means 'city of the gods'.

The Feathered Serpent

Inside the Citadel was the Temple of the Feathered Serpent. It had originally been covered in panels with enormous sculpted heads of feathered serpents sticking out, but only one panel survives. The carved serpent head from the Temple of the Feathered Serpent weighs about 4 tonnes.

The city

Many people lived in Teotihuacan. It was planned with straight but narrow streets lined with groups of houses. It had a large ceremonial centre. A long straight road, now called the Avenue of the Dead, linked a temple called the Pyramid of the Moon with an area now known as the citadel. Halfway along was a another huge temple – the Pyramid of the Sun.

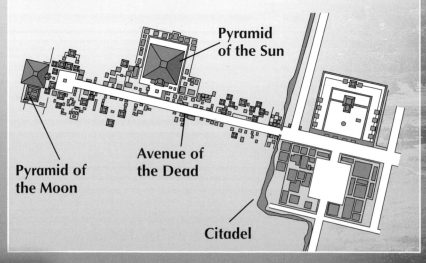

Pyramid of the Sun

Avenue of the Dead

Pyramid of the Moon

Citadel

Offerings to the Feathered Serpent

Archaeologists have found pits at the Temple of the Feathered Serpent containing bones. They were the remains of 120 people who had been sacrificed. Most of them seem to have been warriors. Studies of their bones have shown that the majority were not from Teotihuacan. We do not know why the sacrifices were made or why the feathered serpent sculptures were so important.

The Pyramid of the Sun

The end of the Aztecs

Religion was the centre of Aztec life. When the Spanish appeared in 1519, many people thought Quetzalcoatl, one of the gods, had returned. The Aztecs did not realize the Spanish, led by Hernán Cortés, would soon destroy their mighty empire.

Quetzalcoatl

Quetzalcoatl

The Aztecs believed that the pale-skinned god Quetzalcoatl had gone away to the east – but they also thought he would come back. When the Aztec king Moctezuma II received reports of pale-skinned people who had appeared in the east, he thought that Quetzalcoatl had returned. He sent offerings of treasure to the visitors and invited them to visit his capital.

The god Tonatuih is shown in the centre of this painted stone.

Did You Know?

When the Spanish arrived, so did their diseases. Many people in Tenochtitlan fell ill and died of smallpox.

Spanish conquerors

The pale-skinned people who had arrived in South America in 1519 were Spanish explorers and soldiers. The richness of the Aztecs' offerings made them greedy and they wanted more. When Moctezuma allowed them to enter the city of Tenochtitlan, they took him captive. He was killed in 1520 and the Aztec Empire soon fell apart.

Treasure!

The Spaniards took most of Moctezuma's treasure. Nearly all of it was sent to Spain, where the first shipment arrived in 1520. Some of the Aztec treasure has survived, and can be seen in European museums. Many things just vanished, such as the feathered headdresses (like the modern copy shown here), which some noble Spanish children used for dressing up.

Australia

During the last Ice Age the sea level was much lower than it is now. Australia, New Guinea and Tasmania were joined together, and early people from Asia were able to cross the sea and settle there.

The first people

At first, people settled around the coastline of Australia and up river valleys, from where they explored the land. They were the ancestors of the native Australians, often called Aborigines today.

Cut off?

The planet began to warm up, ice melted and the sea rose. In about 5000 BC, huge areas of coastline were flooded and Australia was cut off from its neighbours. People had to move inland, where conditions could be hard. They moved around in search of food, sometimes settling for a while, and traded with other groups.

Top Facts

- Uluru, once called Ayers Rock, is a sandstone mountain in the Australian desert. It is more than 300 metres high and measures 9 kilometres around the base.

- Differently coloured earths were traded among Aborigine groups. They used the colours for rock paintings.

Big animals

The first people shared the continent with some large animals, such as the giant diprotodon, when they arrived. They do not seem to have hunted them but these very large animals are now extinct. The people chased smaller animals and gathered wild grasses. They lived in shelters formed by overhanging cliffs.

Rock paintings

Early Australian people decorated rocks with beautiful coloured paintings. Many of these still exist. There are handprints, patterns and larger pictures. Sometimes these are of animals and sometimes they are of figures and spirits. These handprints are in a cave in the Bungle Bungle range in Western Australia.

Uluru is one of the most sacred sites for Aborigines in modern times, and might have been equally important for thousands of years.

Acropolis
The centre of a Greek city, often on higher ground

Agora
The central meeting place and market area in a Greek city

Amphitheatre
An oval-shaped building in a Roman city, open to the sky, with seats in rows, one above another, around an open space at ground level. Used for staging gladiator fights

Amphora
A two-handled jar, often with a pointed base, used for transporting liquids such as wine or oil

Amulet
A good luck charm, sometimes in the shape of a god

Aqueduct
A large bridge with a channel for water across the top or a pipe carrying water

Archaeologist
A person who studies the remains of past civilizations

Arena
The middle of a Roman amphitheatre, where contests took place

Atrium
A large open space within a modern building, usually more than one storey high with large windows or a glass roof. In a Roman house the atrium is a central courtyard and has no roof

Dates
Most of the dates given in this book have the letters BC or AD next to them. BC stands for 'Before Christ'; AD stands for 'Anno Domini', which is Latin for 'in the year of the Lord' and is used for dates after the birth of Christ. Some dates in this timeline have a small c. in front of them. That means 'circa', the Latin word for 'about'. It's used when we know roughly when something happened but not the exact date.

BC

c.100,000   The earliest evidence for modern humans in the Near East. People begin moving into what are now Australia and the Americas, making use of land bridges, between about 50,000 and 20,000 years ago

c.30,000–20,000   Major works of art created in European caves such as Lascaux

c.10,500   People settle in Jericho

c.10,000–8000   Farming begins in the Middle and Near East. It has spread throughout Western and Northern Europe by c. 2000 BC

c.8000   Sea levels start rising after the Ice Age, separating North America and Asia, and Asia and Australia. Tasmania is an island by 5000 BC, and many coastal settlements in Australia are under water by then, too

Barbarian
The name the Greeks and Romans gave to the people who lived outside their empires and who spoke other languages

Battering ram
A large beam of wood, used for knocking down walls

Capital
The top of a column, often decorated with carvings

Centurion
A Roman army officer who commanded 80 men

Chariot
A wheeled vehicle, drawn by horses

Citizen
A man who could join in the government of the city (or city state) in which he was born or lived. Slaves could not be citizens

City state
A city which governs itself, with its surrounding territory

Cuneiform
A system of writing developed in Mesopotamia

Democracy
A system of government, originating in Greece, in which citizens choose their leaders

Demotic
A shorthand Egyptian written script

Delta
The triangular area of land where a river meets the sea, such as the Nile Delta

Dynasty
A succession of rulers, often from the same family

---

c.3500 The first cities begin to appear in Mesopotamia

c.3100 King Narmer unites Upper and Lower Egypt

c.3000 A large number of people now live in the Mesopotamian city of Uruk, where written documents are in regular use

c.2580 Building of King Khufu's Great Pyramid in Egypt

c.2500 The royal tombs at Ur are constructed and filled

c.2500–1800 The Indus Civilization develops and flourishes

c.2300 The Akkadian Empire develops in Mesopotamia

c.2150 The rise of the Sumerian Empire, ruled from Ur

c.2000 Stonehenge is under construction in Britain

c.2000–c.1450 The Minoan civilization develops and flourishes on Crete

c.2000 Early evidence of farming, pottery and metalworking in South America

1792–1750 Hammurabi rules Babylon

c.1700 Shang Dynasty kings become rulers of large parts of China

c.1550–1070 Egyptian royal tombs are built in the Valley of the Kings

c.1479 Hatshepsut becomes regent of Egypt

c.1450 Eruption of a large volcano on the island of Thera, not far from Crete

c.1350 The Cretan palace of Knossos is destroyed by fire

Egyptologists
Archaeologists who study ancient Egypt

Embalming
Preserving a dead body using chemicals, ointments and perfumes

Empire
A group of countries or territories controlled by one country

Flint
A smooth, hard rock which can be chipped to obtain a sharp edge or point

Forum
The central open area in a Roman town, used for markets and meetings and often surrounded by official buildings and temples

Gladiator
A man, often a slave or prisoner, who fought others in a Roman amphitheatre. Men who fought animals were called *bestiarii*

Griffin
An imaginary creature with a lion's body but the head and wings of an eagle

Hieratic
A simplified version of Egyptian hieroglyphics

Hieroglyphics
Writing made up of individual picture symbols, used in Ancient Egypt

Hoplite
A Greek foot soldier

Insula
An apartment building in a Roman city

---

c.1327 The death and burial of Egypt's boy king Tutankhamun

c.1250 The construction of the Lion Gate at Mycenae; other Mycenean towns are fortified

c.1250 The possible time of the Trojan War

c.1200 Mycenaean civilization is coming to an end

c.1027 The Zhou Dynasty overthrows the Shang rulers of China

c.1000 Greeks begin to set up colonies outside Greece

c.1000 The Latins first settle in the area of Rome

776 Traditionally the date of the very first Olympic Games

668–627 The Assyrian Empire is at its height under King Ashurbanipal II

612–609 Overthrow of the Assyrian Empire

551 Cyrus II unites the Medes and Persians, beginning the Persian empire by conquering the Empire of Babylon

546 The Persians take over Greek colonies in Ionia (now Turkey)

525 The Persians conquer Egypt

522 Darius I, the Persian ruler responsible for starting to build Persepolis, comes to the throne and expands his empire further

510 The last king of Rome is driven out of the city and the Roman republic is founded

500–499 Greek colonists rebel against their Persian overlords

490 The Persians invade Greece but are beaten at the battle of Marathon

480 Xerxes, king of the Persians, invades Greece again. His progress is delayed at Thermopylae, but he takes Athens. He is defeated at Salamis

Ivory

The hard white material of elephant tusks, often traded in the ancient world

Lapis lazuli

A blue semi-precious stone

Legend

A story that has been told for many, many years, passed down through generations of people. A legend may be true or untrue

Linen

Cloth made from flax plants

Mastaba

A brick tomb in Egypt, used for royal burials before the pyramids were built

Megaliths

Neolithic monuments made using huge stones, mainly in Europe. Stonehenge in England is the most famous example

Mosaic

A design, often found on Roman floors, made from small pieces of stone or tile

Mummy

An embalmed body, often from Egypt

Obsidian

A dark volcanic rock which looks like black glass and which can be shaped to a sharp edge or point

Oracle

A priest or priestess who carried messages from the gods

---

479 The Persians are defeated again at Plataea and thrown out of Greece

449 Work begins on rebuilding the Parthenon in Athens

431–404 The Peloponnesian Wars – Sparta invades, besieges and conquers Athens, but the states then fight between themselves

359 Philip II becomes ruler of Macedonia

338 Philip conquers an alliance of Greek city states

337 Death of Philip II; Alexander succeeds his father

334 Alexander leads his troops into Asia Minor (now Turkey)

333 Alexander defeats the Persian king, Darius II, at Issus and destroys the Persian army at Gargamela. He goes on to conquer many countries including Egypt and marches towards India

323 The death of Alexander in Babylon

c.300 The Maya start to build cities in Central America

241 Sicily is Rome's first territory outside Italy

221 Qin Shi Huangdi becomes the first emperor of China

218 Hannibal, the Carthaginian general, attacks Rome

216 The battle of Cannae; the Romans are defeated by the Carthaginians

210 The death of Qin Shi Huangdi

202 The Carthaginians and their allies are defeated by the Romans, who gain lots of territory and destroy Carthage itself in 146 BC. The Han Dynasty begins in China

107 Marius begins reorganizing the Roman army, making it more professional

Papyrus
A reed used to make a kind of paper. A papyrus is also a document made from papyrus reeds

Patrician
A Roman from one of the noblest families

Plateau
A large area of high, flat land

Plebeian
An ordinary Roman, but definitely a citizen rather than a slave

Pyramid
A huge structure with a square base and sloping slides which meet at the top

Pyramid, stepped
A structure with the same general shape as a pyramid, but made up of layers getting progressively smaller

Regent
Someone appointed to govern temporarily in place of a very young ruler

Republic
A state whose rulers are elected

Rhyton
A Greek container in the shape of an animal head or horn which contained liquids used in religious ceremonies

Sacrifice
An offering or gift made to a god or goddess. Sacrifices could be food, gold or other precious items, but could also involve killing an animal or even a person

---

c.100 Nasca culture begins in South America

58–51 Julius Caesar conquers Gaul for Rome

55 Caesar's troops raid Britain

49 Caesar returns to Rome and seizes power; civil war breaks out

44 The death of Caesar, assassinated in the Senate by a group of republican senators

42 Caesar's killers are defeated at Phillipi by Mark Antony and Caesar's heir, Octavian. They divide the Roman Empire between them.

c.33 Civil war between Mark Antony and Octavian

31 Octavian defeats Mark Antony and Egypt's Queen Cleopatra at Actium; Egypt becomes a part of the Roman Empire

27 Octavian takes the name Augustus after being declared 'first citizen' of Rome. He is effectively its first emperor

AD

c.1–800 Moche culture flourishes in South America

43 Britain is conquered by the Roman armies of the emperor Claudius

64 A huge fire destroys most of Rome

79 The Colosseum is opened in Rome. A huge volcanic eruption destroys Pompeii and Herculaneum

117 The Roman Empire is now at its largest. Hadrian comes to the throne and reduces it to a slightly more manageable size. He fortifies its borders, building Hadrian's Wall across Britain in 122–127

c.200 The Hopewell people build large mounds in Ohio, USA

284 Diocletian becomes Roman emperor and splits the empire into two parts, east and west

c.300–800 The Mayans flourish in Central America

Sarcophagus
A stone tomb or coffin, often decorated

Scribe
Someone who made and kept written records

Silk Road
Ancient trade route linking China, through central Asia and the Middle East, to the Mediterranean and on to Europe

Silt
Fine soil carried along by a river

Slave
A person, man, woman or child, who was owned by someone else. Like any other piece of property, slaves had no rights and could be bought or sold

Sphinx
An Egyptian statue with the body of a lion and the head of a human, often a king, or an animal associated with a god

Strigil
A curved stick used to scrape dirt off the skin in a Roman bath-house

Terracotta
A mixture of clay and sand used to make statues or pottery

Torc
A short necklace or band worn on the arm, made in precious metal

Vizier
An advisor to the Egyptian pharaoh

Ziggurat
A stepped temple in Mesopotamia, with smaller levels on top of larger ones

---

c.300–600 The city of Teotihuacan is thriving in what is now Mexico

312 Constantine becomes emperor of the entire Roman Empire. He moves the capital eastwards to Byzantium in 330

395 The Roman Empire is split once more, permanently this time. The Roman army begins to leave Britain and Gaul about now

402–410 Barbarian tribes invade Italy and reach Rome. They invade Spain in 409

451 Atilla the Hun's barbarian armies are defeated in Gaul by an alliance of Romans and other barbarian tribes

455 More barbarians, the Vandals, invade Italy. They destroy Rome

466 The last Roman emperor in the west is forced into exile. He is defeated by the barbarian leader Odoacer in 476

800 The start of settlements at Chaco Canyon, in New Mexico. Building stops in the 1100s and by the 1200s the Colorado Plateau, including Mesa Verde, has been abandoned

c.1200 The Incas, based at Cuzco, are by now the most powerful people in South America. Their empire expands until the late 1300s, and they are conquered by the Spanish in the 1530s.

c.1325 The founding of the city of Tenochtitlan by the Aztecs

1519 The Spanish arrive in Tenochtitlan

1521 The collapse of the Aztec Empire

1524 Spanish adventurers arrive in what was the centre of Mayan territory.

1532 The Spanish arrive in Peru, and the Inca Empire collapses

ACKNOWLEDGEMENTS

Photo credits
b = bottom, t = top, r = right, l = left, c = centre

Cover images:

Front: tl © Steve Allen/Brand X/Corbis, tc © Bettmann/CORBIS,
tr © Steve Allen/Brand X/Corbis, c © B.S.P.I./CORBIS,
bl © The Gallery Collection/Corbis, br Tim Graham/Getty Images.
Back: tl North Carolina Museum of Art/CORBIS, tr © Richard T. Nowitz/CORBIS,
bc © Richard T. Nowitz/CORBIS.
Spine: Araldo de Luca/CORBIS.

Internal images:

Corbis

1, 2-3, 8-9, 10-11, 12l, 12r, 13, 14-15, 14, 16-17, 16, 17b, 18-19, 22-23, 22t, 22b, 24-25, 24, 25, 26, 27,
29tr, 32-33, 33, 34-35, 34, 36-37, 36, 37t, 37b, 38-39, 38, 39, 40-41, 40t, 40b, 40-41, 41, 42-43, 42,
43t, 43b, 44-45, 45t, 45b, 46-47, 46, 48-49, 48, 49l, 49r, 50-51, 51tl, 51tr, 51b, 52-53, 52, 53t, 53b, 55t,
55b, 56-57, 56, 57, 58-59, 59tr, 59l, 60-61, 60, 61, 62-63, 62, 63b, 64, 65, 66-67, 68-69, 68, 69, 70-71,
70, 72-73, 73, 76-77, 77t, 77b, 78-79, 79, 80, 81, 82, 83, 84-85, 85, 87t, 87br, 87bl, 88-89, 88l, 88r, 89,
90-91, 90, 91, 93t, 93b, 94-95, 95t, 95b, 96-97, 98-99, 99t, 99b, 100-101, 102-103, 102, 103l, 103r,
106l, 106r, 107t, 106-7, 108-109, 108b, 109, 110-111, 110t, 110b, 112-113, 112, 113, 114-115,
116-117, 117, 119, 120-121, 120, 121t, 122-3, 126-127, 128-129, 129b, 130-131, 130, 131, 132-133,
132l, 132r, 134-135, 134, 135, 136-137, 138-139,138, 139t, 140-141, 141, 142, 142-143, 143,
144-145, 144, 145t, 145b, 146, 147b, 148, 149t, 148-149, 150-151, 150, 151tr, 151tl 151b, 152,
,152-153, 153tl, 153r, 154-155, 154, 155, 156, 157, 156-157, 158-159, 161, 162, 162-163, 164-165,
166-167, 167t, 167b, 168-169, 169t, 169b, 170t 170b, 171t 171b, 172-173, 173, 174-175, 174, 175,
176-177, 176, 177, 178-179, 180-181, 181, 182-183,182, 183, 184-185, 185, 188-189, 189b, 190-191,
191, 192-193, 193t, 193b, 194-195, 194, 195, 196, 197, 198-199, 198t, 198b, 200-201, 200, 201,
202-203, 202, 203, 203b, 204-205, 205, 206-207, 207, 208-209, 208, 209, 210-211, 210, 211t, 211b,
212-213, 213, 213b

Getty Images

4-5, 6-7, 12-13, 15, 17t, 20-21, 21t, 26-27, 28-29, 29tl, 30, 32, 47c, 47b, 54-55, 63t, 64-65, 74-75, 74,
75l, 80-81, 86-87,92-93, 92, 97t, 100, 101,118-119, 124-125, 178-179, 180, 189t

GNP
122, 123t, 123b, 127t, 128, 129t, 137c, 147t, 146-7, 157t, 159t, 160

A/w from Parragon: 21b, 29b, 71, 75r , 184, 187